THE CHANGING FACES OF

Cowley

BOOK TWO

Carole Newbigging
and
Trevor Williams

Robert Boyd
PUBLICATIONS

Published by
Robert Boyd Publications
260 Colwell Drive
Witney, Oxfordshire OX8 7LW

First published 1995

Copyright ©
Carole Newbigging
and
Trevor Williams

ISBN 1 899536 04 3

Printed and bound in Great Britain at The Alden Press, Oxford

Contents

Front cover illustration

Rev Georgie Moore, incumbent of Cowley for 53 years, from 1875 to 1928.
'In his clerical dress Mr Moore looked like Robin Hood, so green were his garments. And as he roamed about Cowley he always hummed the same tune that was as musical as a swarm of bees.'

Acknowledgements

The authors are grateful to the institutions, librarians, companies and individuals through whose kindness the photographs in this book were made available. In particular they wish to thank:

The Centre for Oxfordshire Studies Photographic Archives (OPA); the Cowley Local History Society; Oxford & County Newspapers; Kelly's Directories Limited; Nuffield Press; B T Batsford Limited; Austin Rover; Oxfordshire Health Archives; Oxfordshire Guide Executive; Scout Museum; Dyers (Structural Steel) Ltd; Oxford Spiritualist Church. Permitted use has been made of extracts from the following publications. Nuffield Press, *A Jubilee History;* From *Acre End* by Morris Harris, published 1982 Chatto & Windus Ltd.; Pressed Steel Factory, 24 Years of Progress 1926-50.

We acknowledge contribution from so many individuals who made this second book possible. In particular we thank Pete Alder, Mrs Barrett, Mr J Barson, Mrs Cynthia Bateman, Laurie Bates, Bill Beechey, Jim Brand, Sid Brookfield, Cyril Claridge, Mrs Cook, Mrs Una Dean, Jim Dodds, Haydn Evans, Mr T Exler, Mr F Gibbons, Aubrey and Ron Godfrey, Clifford Gooch, Mrs J M Harper, Miss Edna Hartley, Eileen Hawkes, Colin Hobbs, Mrs D Holly, Don Holton, Patrick King, Bill Knights, Richard Linguard, David and Alfred Munday, Glyn Newlands, Roy Payne, Helen Pearson, Neville Rogers, Stan Shergold, Mrs W Sherlock, Mrs K J Smart, Janet Smart, Mrs Audrey Smith, Brenda Sollis, Mrs Steinburg, Jim Tanner, Mrs K Thompson, Mrs L Watts, Brian Weston, Ted Wheelock, Mrs E Williams and Mrs N Windscheffel.

Preface

Following the publication last year of the first *Changing Faces* ... the compilers were asked, many times, why a particular subject, building or family had not been included. Information may have been readily available on a subject, but the book was primarily a photographic record and often photographs were not available, or even known to exist.

Happily, this situation has been resolved for many of our subjects. As a direct result of the book's popularity we have contacted many more people with fascinating memories of Old Cowley. Some of these people were kind enough to lend much treasured photographs and documents, which appeared from the depths of the loft, treasure chests and various shoe boxes under the bed! Original photographs and family snaps are seeing the light of day for the first time for many years. Some of these photographs are in poor condition, some have been kept in wallets for many years and have become well worn. We have, of course, attempted to produce high quality photographs but the collection in this, the second book, relies heavily on private collections and we therefore make no apology for the few of lesser quality that have been included; we believe readers will appreciate the subject matter and the obvious history that is associated with the photograph.

We wanted this second book to be a natural extension to the first, to complement it but also to increase the subjects covered, particularly to record the people and events of Cowley as well as the buildings that have changed over the years. Hence, we have a section entitled Cowley Families and Characters, which has been fascinating to record. Needless to say, readers will be aware of others who should have been included in this category. It may be that we were not aware of these characters, or that we were unable to contact present day family or to obtain a photograph. Another important section, we feel, is the VE and VJ day celebrations, fronted by the Roll of Honour from St James Church. We felt it appropriate for a book being published in 1995, the 50th anniversary of the end of World War II, to commemorate these events.

Wherever possible information has been checked, but human memory is not infallible and the dating of photographs is sometimes very difficult. We strive for accuracy, but a few errors are inevitable — we trust it does not detract from the overall enjoyment of this, the Second Collection.

We dedicate this book to everyone who has ever lived or worked in Cowley, in particular those men and women of Cowley who served their country both in the forces and at home either working on the land, in the factories or within the Home Guard.

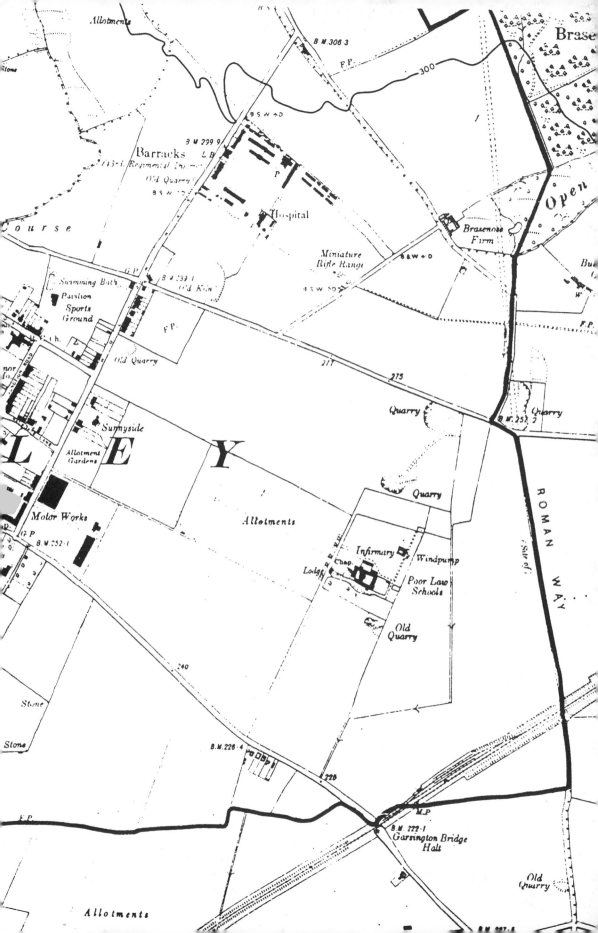

Parish Boundaries

Ethelred's charter of 1004 describes the bounds of Cowley as enclosing three hides of land '... *the bounds in so far as they are intelligible include a large part of the present Cowley: from Cherwell Bridge eastward by Haklingcroft to a brook, round to Hockmore, then to Iffley, back to the brook, and then back to the Cherwell'.*

During the next nine hundred years the boundaries changed several times. Maurice Beauchamp, Vicar of Cowley, defined the boundaries in the Cowley Church Parish Magazine of 1935. *'As we go visiting we find that many of those who have lately come into the Parish think that they are living either in Iffley or Headington, because they have to have Iffley or Headington put on their letters. But this is simply a postal arrangement and has nothing to do with the actual boundaries of the Parish. In order to make this clear let me give you what are the actual boundaries of Cowley.*

On the Eastern side the Slade is the boundary, and the boundary continues down Brasenose Lane to the railway line, along the Horspath Road the boundary is the Railway, along the Garsington Road the boundary is again the Railway. Going into Oxford the Brook is the boundary on the left-hand side, but on the other side the Parish extends to Cumberland Road, the side nearest the Bus Company being in Cowley, the other side not being in Cowley, and although Glanville Road is in Cowley, Southfield School is just over the boundary. On the Iffley side all Florence Park and Westbury Crescent is in Cowley, and the greater part of Rose Hill, along the London Road the boundary is Clarke's Garage, on the other side of the road all the new building that is going on behind 'The Allied Arms' is in the Parish of Cowley as far as the Council houses. The Council houses, however, are in the Parish of Iffley. The new Somerset, Barnes Court and Cruel Lane estates are all in Cowley.

This will give you an idea of the extent of the Parish and the tremendous growth in population which is taking place. Cowley has the largest population of any in the City and within about the first three in the Diocese.'

Cowley at War

St James's Church, the parish church of Cowley, had within its parish Cowley Barracks, built 1874, the headquarters of the Oxfordshire Light Infantry (OLI). The church was the regimental chapel of the OLI until 1908 when the regiment was amalgamated with the Buckinghamshire Light Infantry to form the Oxon and Bucks Light Infantry (OBLI). St James's Church contains memorials to the OLI and to its own parishioners who died in the 1914-18 War (73 names) and in the 1939-45 War (86 names).

In memory of the Cowley Men who laid down their lives in the Great War 1914-18.

Capt E H Kirkpatrick, OBLI   Capt R O Logan, OBLI
Capt R R M Brooke, OBLI   Capt C F K Carfrae OBLI
Capt Jack Manley RFC   2nd Lieut J S C Marshall OBLI

Albert Alder	James Conolly	Wilfred King
Leslie Allen	Herbert Cook	William Knapp
Sidney Allen	Reginald Doubleday	John E C McClusky
Cyril Atkins	George Druce	William Merritt
Alfred Attwood	Frederick Edgington	William Mitchel
Alfred Bancalari	William Edgington	Harold Morris
Arthur Baker	Claude George	Thomas Neighbour
James Baker	Charles Gibbon	Harry Owen
Ronald Baughan	Edward Goodgame	Harold Peake
Reginald Belcher	Gabriel Greenfield	Frank Phipps
John Biggs	Arthur Grey	Leonard Reynolds
Fredk Borough	Frederick Hall	Herbert Rogers
Alfred Bradbury	William Harris	William Rogers
George Brandish	Frederick Harvey	John Henry Rogers
Fredk Brockall	William Hazell	Leonard Smith
Arthur Brown	Cecil Hilsdon	Alfred States
Sidney Brown	Edward Huson	William Trinder
William Brown	Aubrey Johnson	Frederick Viner
Frank Butler	Jesse Jones	Harry Wallin
Jeremiah Currell	Joseph Kent	Hubert Weston
Alfred Carter	Jack King	Henry Winter
William Cobb	Oliver King	James Young

Roll of Honour

Dedicated to the Memory of the Men of Cowley
Who gave their lives for their Country
in the Great War of 1939-45 and the Falklands in 1982

Ashfield J	Bailey W	Beecham M S. (RAF)
Birmingham C (OBLI)	Birt A	Bishop C
Bowles P H (RA)	Brown E R (OBLI)	Brown S
Burrell D	Burrell P	Burchell P (RAF)
Cambray B	Carter F	Cato N
Coomber A	Cooper N (RAF)	Cripps T
Curtis H	Daultrey L	Day D
Earl G	Elder V	Flexon R
Florey A (RA)	Florey G (OBLI)	Ford J C (RAF)
Foulkes C (RN)	France R	Franklin A J (RAF)
Franklin W (RWK)	Frith E	Fryer A R (RAOC)
Fuller E J (RN)	Garner G	Gibbons R
Giles A C (RAF)	Gomershall R	Gooch E
Green H	Haynes S	Hazell C
Hibbet L	Hicks C	Hicks L
Hill G	Hilsdon V (RAF)	Hollis J
Holmes R	Holt J	Hulton K
Keen R	Kent F	Kerry A (RA)
King G	Knights P (RAF)	Kyme C
Laurie L	Lipscombe R (OBLI)	Luther W
McCarthy J	Martin R	Moore G
Morgan E (OBLI)	Morris D	Nattrass W
Paget F	Parker K (RAF)	Perry D
Pickering G (RAF)	Plaister R (REME)	Price F C (RAF)
Probitts L	Rees W	Shead W (OBLI)
Stannard W	Taylor A	Thomas H C S (RAF)
Thompson J	Thurley R	Webb A
Whalley J (RAF)	Whitbread B	White V
Withers D	Young B	Hall (RN) (Falklands)

Both Morris Motors and Pressed Steel Company were turned over to war time production. *'Products included bodies for military vehicles and aircraft frames, sea mines, baby respirators to cope with gas attacks, steel helmets, jerricans, land mines, gun cartridge cases and ammunition boxes in vast quantities.'*

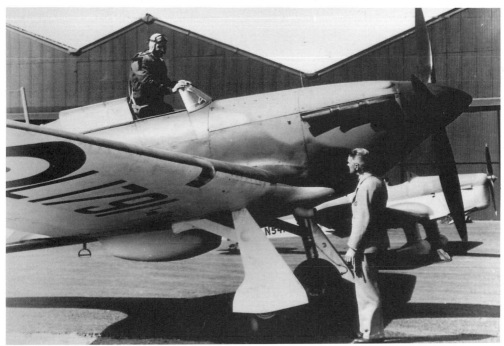

Outside the Flight Sheds at Cowley, a rebuilt Hurricane with the test pilot talking to Lord Nuffield.

William Morris was the power behind the establishing of No 1 Civilian Repair Unit at a vital time just at the outbreak of war. The car despatch department on the south side of Garsington Road became a giant hangar and workshop, and the 'car men turned air mechanics' set to, making their tools as they went, with very little experienced leadership to show them how. The factory specialised in Spitfires and Hurricanes and during the Battle of Britain minor battle-damaged aircraft were often sent direct from battle to Cowley, which soon became known to the pilots as the 'Outpatients Department'.

Associated with this activity was No 50 Maintenance Unit, which was a recovery system of crashed aircraft, operated by gangs of old Morris Motors tradesmen, each gang with a mobile workshop. These men would go out in all weathers to recover crashed aircraft, which were then dismantled in situ and loaded on to 60 foot long articulated lorries, known as 'Queen Mary transporters'. Those deemed recoverable would go to the relevant repair unit and those scrapped to the 'Dump'.

The Dump was probably the biggest scrap yard the area has ever seen. Its working title was the Metal and Produce Recovery Depot, but it was better known as MPRD. This was an area of what were open fields, filled with wrecked aircraft of all nationalities to a considerable height, waiting to be stripped and melted down to aluminium ingots. This Dump stretched from what is now Roman Way along the Garsington Road towards Garsington.

Aircraft awaiting repair at the hangers at Morris Motors

Four NAAFI girls at the Cowley
Barracks.

Women at war: rivetting Lancaster bomber wings at the Pressed Steel Factory

'Then the Second World War came along and that altered production altogether. First the whole factory had to be blacked out, and that was a mammoth job too. All through the war we made light vehicles for military use — Tiger Moth 'planes (forty a week when we really got going), naval torpedoes, wireless for the searchlight batteries, tripods for machine guns, tail units for Horsa gliders, power plants, Lancaster and that, jerry cans and helmets and land mines — you name it, we made it.' (Chatto and Windus)

A secret drawing office in the Poplars, the Cowley Industrial School, and the prototype of a submarine. The War finished before this went into production.

The Morris Motors Home Guard in 1942.

VE Day Parties:

Clive Road.

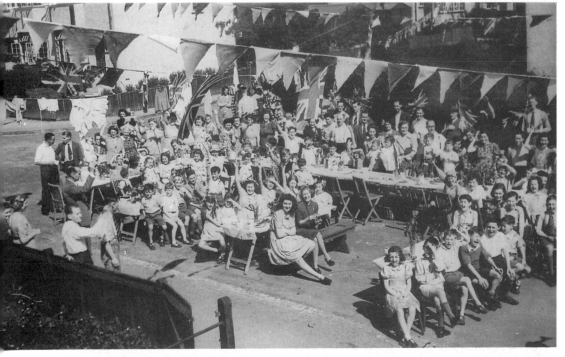

Cleveland Drive, with St Omer Road and Gerard Place.

Temple Road celebrations.

Kelburne Road at the Queens Arms. Left to right back row: -?-, -?-, -?-, Mrs Mathews, Mrs Hayes, Mrs Gaisford, Mrs Braggington, Mrs Thomas, Mrs Gillies, Bertha Wilmot (Landlady), -?-, -?-, -?-, Mrs Brewer, -?-, Mrs Threadkill, -?-, Mrs Stickley.

White Road was extremely hectic.

Crescent Road.

Dodgson Road residents joined forces with Liddell Road and Barns Road for celebrations which included a puppet show.

Children celebrating VE day outside the Nuffield Arms in Bartholomew Road.

Cowley Families and Characters

Over the years Cowley has boasted many colourful characters. Some will be well remembered to many Cowley people, others may be just a distant memory, while a few may be no more than a family legend. Here we remember just some of them.

PC 'Jim' Brand, 1912 - 1982

One of the best remembered characters of Cowley during the 1940s and '50s was the local constable, PC Ralph Brand, but always known as 'Jim', who lived at Brasenose Driftway. His imposing figure was a deterrent to the young children of Cowley and, if any mischief was imminent, and he was spotted, the cry of *'Watch it, here comes Copper Brand'* would be heard. Seeing school children safely across the road and controlling the works traffic at the junction of Hollow Way and Oxford Road were amongst his more obvious duties. He joined the force in 1936 and in 1958 received a Commendation Medal for arresting four men in the City single-handed.

The Cowley Dwarfs.

Emily and George Godfrey, affectionately known as the Cowley Dwarfs, were born in Hockmore Street in 1880 and 1883, part of a large family. Their father was Charles Godfrey, a wheelwright and coffin maker who worked for Mr Bancalari at the top of Crescent Road, and their mother Emma White, and they were part of a large family. Emily is remembered as having long red hair; George was often to be found *'sitting on the arches over the Cowley Brook, where his legs did not touch the ground'*, and as an adult he liked to sport a flower in his lapel.

The photograph above was taken during the 1890s: George on the left with his father, Charles, mother Emma on the right with Emily. Gladys, daughter of older brother Frank, is in the centre.

Outside 28 The Marsh, where they lived with their sister, Eva.

The Reverend Georgie Moore, Vicar of Cowley, 1875-1928

Love him or hate him, you could not ignore him! Georgie Moore made his presence felt in Cowley for over 50 years. His funeral in May 1928 was well attended, with representatives from the Cowley Barracks and many local dignitaries.

He was very fond of children and was responsible for the management of the local church schools, the choir, the Sunday School outings and many more children's activities.

George Moore was more than a match for his parishioners. He farmed 600 acres, and was known as the Farming Vicar of Cowley, and his preference for settling any dispute there and then with his fists led him twice to be summonsed for assault, in his own churchyard, before he had been in the parish ten years.

Herman Francis Munday
1902–1968

Herman Munday was born at Waterstock in 1902, the youngest of a family of eight, and was educated at the village school, John Hampden School in Thame, and Lord William's Grammar School, Thame. From there he went to Culham College to train as a school master 1921-23.

His first post was at Littlemore Mixed School where, after one year, he was appointed headmaster at the young age of twenty two. In 1925 he married Ivy Kate Smart, who had been a schoolmistress at Cowley Girls School. Appointed to the staff of Temple Cowley Senior School in 1932 as Deputy Headmaster, he served there for more than thirty years until his retirement in 1963.

He had many enthusiasms, but high amongst them was scouting. It was in 1925 that he formed the 1st Littlemore (Lone) Troop of Scouts, later the 28th Oxford. Coun. E J Phipps, then scoutmaster of the 19th, sent him Cyril J Tibbetts, later to become an Assistant Commissioner and life long friend, to show him the ropes. Other troops he formed were the 44th troop (Temple Cowley Senior School) and the 45th troop (Temple Cowley Congregational Church). He was Assistant District Commissioner for Oxford, and awarded the Medal of Merit and Silver Wolf by the Scout Movement.

Football was another major interest. He managed school and adult teams (The City Colts) and was active for forty years with 'Oxford Schools Football Association' as Chairman and President. He had outstanding successes with his school teams and the City Colts won 28 out of 29 matches in one season, only losing to the City Teachers.

His other interests were numerous: horticulture; a keen beekeeper, with hives at school and at home; a great collector of cigarette cards having at one time 55,000 in his collection; tenor in St Luke's choir from the day it opened in 1938, and a keen scientist and mathematician studying for a B.Sc in his spare time! He was also a member of many committees, including the local Alice Smith Trust for many years, and taught boys and girls astronomy for the Duke of Edinburgh Award Scheme.

Reginald Heward Smith
1901–1982

Reg Smith, centre, with the Prime Minister, Harold Macmillan, at the Cowley Conservative Club in December 1959.

Reg Smith, known as the unchained mayor of Cowley, was particularly well known in the area. His father, Sidney Smith, was friend to Billy Morris — later Lord Nuffield — and there is a popular story in the Smith family of how the young Billy Morris took a fancy to Alice Simmonds, but Alice made her choice and married Sidney! The family lived at Temple Road opposite St Christopher's School, where Alice opened a shop in her front room. The Rev. Georgie Moore was the landlord *'and on rent days he rode down the road running his riding whip along the railings and the tenants came out to him.'* Alice later became a lady's maid and accomplished needlewoman, dressing her children in off-cuts of velvet and satin!

Reg was the eldest surviving child and attended St Christopher's School. He was always interested in sport and was secretary to the Cowley football club, the Lillywhites, and used to visit all the local sporting events with two great friends, Reg King and Frank Bird, all three on one motor bike. Reg joined the Oxford Times as an office boy where he worked for 47 years, eventually becoming Racing Editor and Assistant Sports Editor. He was Secretary, later Chairman then President of Cowley Conservative Club and was a Councillor for Cowley for three years. He was a Trustee of the Elder Stubbs charity and a keen member of the Foresters.

Cheddar Wilson
1900–1981

'Cheddar' Wilson preparing for another swim at Long Bridges, off the Donnington Bridge.

Frank Harold 'Cheddar' Wilson was born at West Street, Osney and attended St Frideswide's school. He soon made his mark in Oxford football by playing for Oxford Boys in the 1913-14 season. After the first world war he joined St Frideswide's - 'The Vicar's Angels' as they were then called. After three years he joined the Cowley Lillywhites where he was a valued player. He is probably best remembered for his fondness of swimming, something he did almost on a daily basis, and celebrated his 70th birthday by swimming from Folly Bridge to Iffley - 2552 yards in a time of 70 minutes - in the annual Oxford Police Sports and Social Club swim, a feat that he often repeated on chilly Christmas mornings! He is also remembered for his love of poetry and ability to recite Shakespeare at every opportunity. 'Cheddar' died at the age of 81 at his home at Blackbird Leys.

Winnum and Wearum

Mention must be made of this well-known, but shadowy, character. Many people will remember him and his chest full of medals which gave him his name - *'I won um and I'll wear um'*. This gentleman was a Mr Bateman who lived at 124 Crescent Road.

Silas Turner—*the Cowley carrier*
1853-1925

Born at Aynho in Oxfordshire, Silas Turner moved to Cowley at the turn of the century with his wife Susan and settled at 98 Crescent Road. Initially he was associated with the Military College, and then set up business as an agent for the Great Western Railway and Haulage Contractor. He also kept a few pigs on land that is now City View Estate, off Crescent Road. They had four children: Harold, William, Susan (Cis) and John.

Harold Turner c1913, with an early Wolsey car

Silas's son, Harold, lived at 45 Crescent Road with his wife Ruth and two children, Audrey and Bill, moving to number 98 in 1933. He took over the haulage business and expanded the pig farm after the first world war. Pigs were born at the bottom of the field, weaned, and then taken to sties at the top. When old enough they were herded across the road to the yard adjoining 98 Crescent Road where they were fattened and supplied to local butchers, mainly Mr Hatt and Mr Harper. Harold played a prominent part in local affairs. He was a member of the Parish Council, one-time President and Chairman of the Cowley Conservative Club, and also a pioneer in the setting up of the Cowley Workers Social Club, of which he became President. His wife, Ruth, was a Secretary of the Primrose League, a branch of the Conservative Association.

Audrey and Bill Turner astride one of the cart horses outside 45 Crescent Road c1929. The horses were stabled on the pig farm and also in the yard adjoining 98 Crescent Road.

Bill Turner herding pigs across the field in the early 1940s. The building in the background is Morris Motors Shooting Range.

The Gibbons family, *Cowley bakers and publicans*

Richard Gibbons and family outside the Cricketers Arms in the 1890s. Left to right back row: George Gibbons (joined the Navy and died in America), Mary Gibbons known as Polly who married Albert Painter, Richard Gibbons and his wife Emily Clegham, Richard, William, Lilian, Thomas and Kate.

Albert Painter married Mary Gibbons and lived opposite the Cricketers Arms in Temple Road until 1908. Their three daughters were Violet Kate, May Emily and Lilian Edith.

The bakehouse and shop on the corner of Between Towns Road and St Omer Road

A Gibbons family group taken 1952 at the bakehouse at Between Towns Road. Left to right at back: Joyce Gibbons, Lawson Adams, Bill Gibbons, Joyce Gibbons, John Deacon, Rita Deacon, George Gibbons, Rose Gibbons, Frederick Gibbons, Dick Gibbons, Mary Gibbons. Next row: Baby Beverley Gibbons, Kitty Gibbons, Dolly Adams, Mrs Matilda Gibbons, Walter Gibbons, Bill Adams. Next row: Arlene Gibbons, Kathy, Jean Gibbons, Kathrine Gibbons, John Gibbons, Margaret Gibbons. Children: Jackie Reynolds, Tony Gibbons, Richard Gibbons, Beverley Gibbons, Roy Gibbons, Hazel Deacon, Janet Gibbons, Ann Adams, Mark Gibbons.

Charles Gibbons started a bakehouse in Salegate Lane, off Temple Road, in 1852, then moved to premises behind the Cricketers Arms. His brother Walter Thomas Gibbons (always known as Tom) joined the bakery at the age of 17 and it was the custom for Charles to bake for the military and for Walter to serve the village.

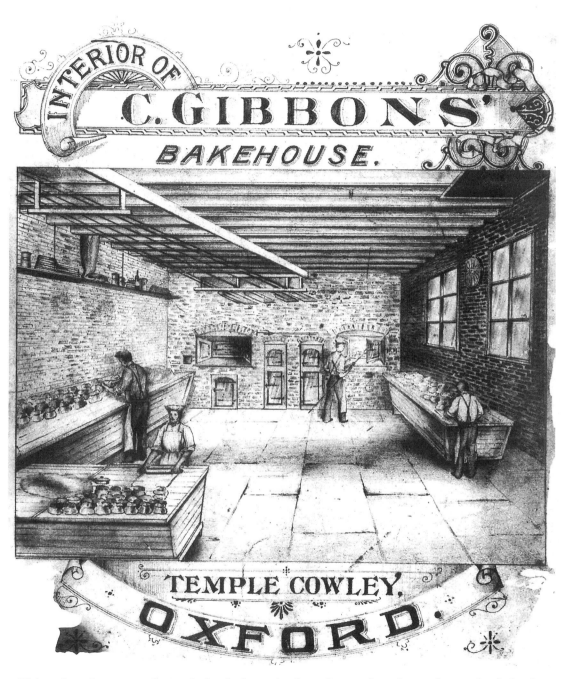

This advertisement plate of the bakery is thought to date from the end of the last century. The bakery stood approximately where the garage now stands in Between Towns Road (OPA)

The Cowley Twins

Sylvia and Cynthia Hinton are well known in Cowley, having worked at the Nuffield Press for over 38 years. They are totally identical in every way. They were made redundant on 11 February 1992 and since that time have been prominent members of the Maxwell Pensioners' Action Group.

Eli Smart, always known as Jack, started an undertaking business in outhouses at the rear of Bartlemas Cottage, later moving to premises at the corner of Hendred Street (then called George Street) and Oxford Road, now the Co-operative Funeral Home. This wedding in 1905 shows Eli and his wife either side of the bride and groom, Jessie North and Willie Smart. Left to right back row: Dolly Smart with husband Bill Slingsby, Elizabeth Jane Smart, Harry Smart, Philip James Smart with wife Clara (nee Smart), Tom Smart, George North being one of the two younger lads, the other unknown. Middle row: Grace and Fred North, Eli, Jessie North, Willie Roland Smart, Francis Annie Smart (nee Parrott), unknown lady. Front: Gertie North, Ivy Smart (later married to Herman Munday), May Smart. The family lived at 20 Southfield Road, where the photo may have been taken.

SECTION THREE

Schools

'Train up a child in the way he should go:
And when he is old, he will not depart from it.'

This saying was a favourite maxim in the days of Miss Symes, infant school mistress and a close friend of the Rev George Moore, and a prominent figure in village life over eighty years ago. *'The mistress's progress to school every morning took the form of a dignified procession. The roads carried little traffic; the few carts moving at the same pace as pedestrians, and cycles were not numerous. So, she walked in the road sweeping up the children as she went along until the numbers swelled to vast proportions and filled the width of the road'.* Cowley Chronicle 1972.

A school pageant at Temple Cowley School c1936.

Temple Cowley school opened on 10 January 1933, to provide secondary education for the children of Cowley's growing industrial population; the school at first replacing the senior sections of the old Church schools of Cowley, Littlemore and Iffley

The Vicar of Cowley played an important part in the management of the local church schools, St James's and St Christopher's. Schools were regularly visited by the School Inspector and these reports, and subsequent prizes, were reported in the parish magazine.

The Cowley Church Parish Magazine for April 1929 reported the following prizes:

Boys School:

Bishops Prize: Maurice Smith. *Certificates:* Cyril Timbs and Joseph Simpson. *Commended (Upper Group):* H Hogan, W Herbert, A Blakeman, H Bowerman, F Crook, J Hartley. *Commended (Middle Group):* P Biggs, C Augar, E Yerbury, F Harbut, C Gardner, D Johnson, W Quartermain, G Hedge. *Commended (Lowest Group):* J Pether, V Spiers, R Aldridge, L Truelove, K Crofts, J Tully, W Payne, P Goodwill, A Turley, R Bonner.

Girls School:

Upper Group Bishops Prize: Doris Lewis. *Certificates:* Nora Stringer, Bertha Whyte. 'I do not feel justified in commending any others as the standard was very poor'. *Commended:* V Allen, G Quartermain, M Huntley, E Allport, G Talbot, B Saxton. *Middle Group: Commended:* R Wheatley, A Flexon, G Bowerman, B Hebborn, G Walters, B Payne, J Clements. *Lowest Group:* 'Quite a good class, well up to standard.' *Commended:* O Wiggins, O Harris, M Rogers, J Hartland, R Buckingham, G White, E Baker.

Infants School:

Commended (First Class): May Everett, Winnie Bruton, Eileen Augar, Brian Foulks, Dennis Hill. *Commended (Second Class):* Jack Dawson, Charles Berry, Thomas Buckingham, Joyce Phipps, Eileen Hebborn. *Commended (Third Class):* H Grimshaw, B Gomm, G Sykes, F Parker, T Willoughby, W Williams, M Steels, E Shirley. Commended (Fourth Class): J Leen, J Anderson, Z Church, R Willis, W Hebborn, C Bishop.

St James's School Std III c1928. Left to right back row: -?-, Tom Shirley, Greenfield, Fred Turrell, Grimshaw. In front of master: Don Holt, King. 3rd row: Anderson, Robin Bonner, Bradbury, Radbone, -?-, Price, Owen, Sonnie Barker. 2nd row: Fred Gibbons, Eden, Paine, -?-, Alf Badger. Front row: -?-, Walter Morris, -?-, -?-, Jack Bartlett, Ronnie Simpson, Frank Godfrey.

St James's School Football Team 1930-31 — Winners of the Shield. Left to right back row: Grimshaw, Ted Taylor, Bill Quarterman, Hicks, Frank Quarterman. Middle row: Turley, -?-, Mr Harris, Richardson, Horace Kitchen. Front row: Ernie Lee, Ken Crook.

St James's School 1937. Left to right back row: Lionel Crook, Royston Titcombe, John Gayton, Leonard Marsh, Alan Glenfield, -?-, Tony Collins, Gordon Martin, Brynmor Evans, Peter Godden, Dennis Payton, Patrick King. Front row: Mark Tasker, -?-, Francis Elders, Charles Hinton, Stanley Windridge, Frederick Ramsden.

St Christopher's School c1927. Left to right front row: -?-, Payne, C Price, -?-, -?-, Surman, Godfrey. 2nd row: -?, T Coomber, D Holton, F Coomber, -?-, Greenfield, T Rogers, A Turley. Back row: -?-, -?-, F Flexon, -?-, R Bonner, -?-, Barker(?), J Hillsdon.

St Christopher's School Football Team 1935, Junior Schools Final played at the White House Ground. Left to right back row: Dennis Kimber, Geoff Gibbons, Ken Halsey, Henry Lay, Frank Taylor. Middle row: Sid Bunce, Ron Buckingham, Edgar Buckingham, Cyril Claridge, James Jarvie. Front row: Tony Harper, Ken Gooch.

St Christopher's Swimming Team: Inter-School Gala Winners 1953. Left to right back row: Richard Farmer, Margaret Butler, Bernard Johnson, Barbara Priest, Robin Cox, Wendy Brooks, Michael Goodman. Front row: Valerie Hall, Ron Wyatt, Pat Ellis, Geoff Underwood, -?-.

St Christopher's Athletic Team: Inter-School Sports Winners 1955. Left to right back row: -?-, Teresa Huddy, Derek Knight, -?-, Richard Farmer, Janice Smith, Paul Mitchell, -?-, Tony Bradbury, Veronica McAvoy. 2nd row: Pete Aries, Sandra Surman, -?-, Jim Simpkins, -?-, Richard Clements, Carole Lowe, David Ivings, Hooper, Jennifer Gibbs. 1st row: Barry Dubber, Stannina Watts, John Hudgell, Sue Bannister, Clive Davis, Sue Wheeler, Trevor Williams, Christopher Brogden. Front row: -?-, Audrey Carter, -?-, -?-, Peter Hines, Rita Aldis, -?-.

Temple Cowley Gymnastic Team c1956. Left to right back row: Clive Davis, Ian Rundle, John Inston, Tony Bradbury, Trevor Williams, Michael Edminson, Graham Weston, Roger Tyler, David Ivings, Steven Quigley, John White, Dave Sawyer. Front row: Malcolm Jenkins, Anthony Cross, Peter Barratt, Gordon McMasters, -?-, Tony Haugh, Mick Hiorns.

Temple Cowley School Scouts c1957. Left to right back row: Ted Tolputt, Michael Childs, Denis McAvoy, Don Pocock, Steve Quigley, Antony Cross, Ian Rundle, Victor Veale, Pete Smith, Trevor Williams, Herman Munday (Scout Master). Middle row: 'Monty' Barratt, Peter Faulkner. Front row: Percy Prytherch, -?-, Malcolm Jenkins, David Childs, Richard Cockhead, Peter Barratt.

Donnington School 4th Year 1949: Left to right back row: Ray Bellinger, John Paulkner, Guilmore, Parkinson, -?-, Mr Busby, Joyce Armstrong, (5 girls unknown). 3rd row: -?-, T Collet, -?-, Peter Bowles, D Scarsbrook, -?-, D Guest, -?-, -?-, Wendy Barnet, -?-. 2nd row: (5 girls unknown), Ann Morse, -?-, Tony Guest, Lionel Fort, Ken McMinn, Jim Dodds. Front row: -?-, Joan Reeves, Sue Ballard, -?-, Ann Morse, Tony Brown, T Lawton, Eric Farr, R Houghton, -?-.

Donnington School Under 11s Football team — Runners Up 1949. Left to right back row: Max Cherry, Tony Collet, D Wheatley, Ray Houghton, Tony Guest, Jim Dodds, Terry Lawton, Hugh Allen. Middle row: Chris Newbold, Alan Wilmer, Eric Farr, Tom Harris, Donald Stewart. Front row: Lionel Fort, Roger Lindsay.

Donnington School Recorder Group, years 3 and 4, during the 1950s.

'Southfield is the first secondary school built by the Oxford Education Committee. It was designed on modern lines, giving the greatest possible amount of light and air. It was built during the period of economy and thus is severely simple in construction, costing only £84 per place. But the greatest care was taken, under the expert hand of the architect, to make every detail simple, appropriate and good of its kind. The colours of the rooms and the design of the furniture were thought out as part of a coherent scheme. The buildings provide accommodation for a two-stream school of 300-350 boys and was so designed that additional class-rooms and practical rooms could readily be built if it is later necessary to accommodate three streams. The school stands on a 16-acre site which will be laid out as playing fields and the Committee have safeguarded another 12 acres against future developments.'

Southfield fused together two elements: the Oxford Municipal Secondary School in S Ebbes and the Oxford Selective Central School for Boys at Gloucester Green, with numbers in the proportion of about two boys from the former to one from the latter.

Southfield School started in the Autumn term of 1934, with a formal opening by Mr H A L Fisher, Warden of New College, on 27 June 1935. In 1964 it amalgamated with the City of Oxford Boys High School, to form Oxford Boys School.

Southfield School nearing completion in 1934.

Southfield School Sea Scouts c1936, taken in front of the school. Mr N Teasdale, master, Mr H Slater and Mr J Alldis, teacher and scout master, are seated on the front row.

Southfield School, Rugby First XV, 1935-6. Back row: D A Templeton, K J Skinner, D S Calcutt, N. C Teasdale, T Dodgson R H Leibermann, J W Welch. Middle row: D A Howard, R. L Brooks, T A Cox, W J Gibbs, W E J Rees, E R Wiblin, N A Gidney. Front pair: H G Phizackerly and N F Granger.

Roll of Honour

1939 - 1945

*

This is the complete Roll of Honour, compiled from our records. Included are the names of those whose obituaries appear in this issue. The publication of these has been delayed in some cases in order that confirmation might be received before recording in the Roll of Honour those Old Boys who had been posted as 'Presumed Killed'.

*

W. A. Wood	19–22		R. A. Stevens	30–36
J. A. Glover	19–25		H. C. S. Thomas	30–36
M. F. Goddard	21–25		K. J. Skinner	31–36
			W. H. Cole	32–36
E. A. Milliner	19–26		F. Morris	32–36
			R. P. Williams	33–36
			R. E. Jennings	35–36
E. B. B. Walker	23–27			
J. W. Bowen	23–27		N. A. Gidney	30–37
			P. G. Burrell	31–37
D. G. Shorey	23–28		A. W. Fletcher	32–37
W. L. Edmunds	24–28		L. A. Hibbett	32–37
			C. H. Leonard	32–37
A. M. Birt	28–29		H. H. Richardson	32–37
L. Kelly	28–29		G. C. Brown	33–37
			G. R. Sugar	33–37
A. J. Frost	24–30		J. E. Boustead	34–37
H. F. Green	25–30		E. R. Turrill	35–37
G. E. Allison	26–30			
C. G. Andrews	26–30		G. P. Chaundy	32–38
E. Tureczek	26–30		J. R. Newman	33–38
E. J. Hicks	27–30		B. M. Luckett	35–38
E. T. C. Frith	28–30		O. B. Norwood	35–38
C. A. Davis	28–31		E. Bourton	34–39
			G. W. Crawley	34–39
L. J. Allum	28–32		G. Hern	34–39
R. A. Keen	28–32		M. E. Owens	34–39
J. Thackham	28–32		J. S. Tubb	34–39
R. G. Longshaw	29–32		P. J. Withers	34–39
D. P. Williams	29–32		B. P. Bailey	35–39
S. Coshall	31–32		P. S. Barnett	35–39
			T. Hitchcock	35–39
C. J. Brock	29–33		P. Knights	35–39
C. M. Wesson	30–33			
			D. E. J. Bint	34–40
W. C. Liebermann	34		F. G. Mathews	35–40
K. G. Silvester	31–34		A. R. Walton	36–40
C. E. T. Wood	31–34			
F. B. Paget	33–34		N. J. Morley	35–41
K. L. F. Parker	30–35		E. R. Dance	37–42
T. A. Hands	31–35			

Southfield School Roll of Honour.

Southfield School staff 1935. Back row: P E Heafford, J L R Aldis, N C Teasdale. Middle row: O R Slater, T Hopkins, F E Dyke, R Freebairn-Smith, H W Spicer, R B Kohler, R McCourty, F Baldwin. Front row: J H Brashour, J S Hill, D G Perry, A H Flemming (Head Master), S J Brookfield, A S Treves, Miss C E Holliday.

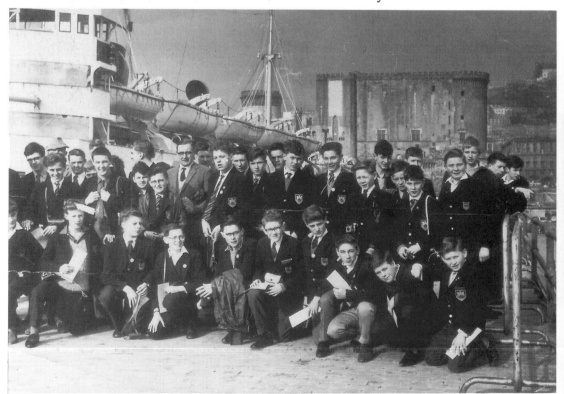

Combined trip for Southfield School and High School — a cruise on the Dunera. Photograph taken 1961 in Naples.

SECTION FOUR

Demolition and Development

Drastic changes took place in Cowley during the early 1960s when Hockmore Street was completely demolished to make way for the new Cowley Shopping Centre, now Templars Square. Between Towns Road was realigned and extended and gradually the shops that were well known to the residents of Cowley were replaced by large office blocks.

'On the site at the moment it seems to be mainly a matter of destruction, and this is bound to be sad, especially for those people who have had to leave their homes, in some cases the houses they were born in, or lived in from childhood.' Cowley Chronicle November 1960.

Barns Road maisonettes, the new Cowley, standing cheek to jowl with Bedford House, the old Cowley, c1960. (Courtesy of Oxford & County Newspapers)

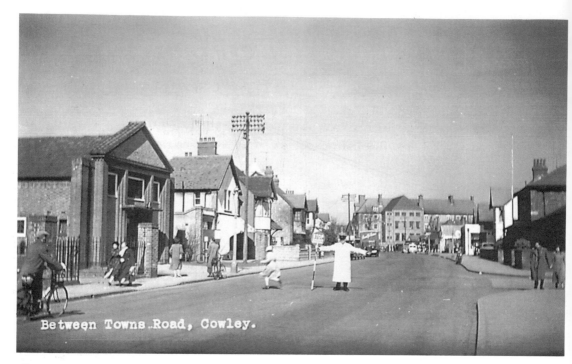

Between Towns Road c1950. St James's Parish Hall was used as an annex for St Christopher's Junior school. The school crossing patrol man is Mr Timms. Nuffield Press, the former Oxford Military College, can be seen in the background.

Numbers 170 and 172 Oxford Road Cowley in the 1960s. Once occupied by the infant school teacher, Miss Knott, now the site of the Cowley Police Station. (OPA)

Number 23 Hockmore Street — a substantial farmhouse owned by Mr Phipps.

This Elizabethan barn belonged to Phipps Farm.

Hockmore Farm stood near Gaisford Road

A photograph of 1868 showing the Windows family who lived in this unusual building, known as Bullingdon Castle, on Barracks Lane, at the back of what is now Morris Motors Social Club. Remnants of the wall are still standing (OPA).

White's Farm at the corner of Temple Road and Oxford Road. This family had lived in Cowley for many generations and were substantial landowners, including land which was later developed as the Pressed Steel Company. (OPA)

Photo c1970 showing numbers 16 and 18 Oxford Road on the corner of Hendred Street. Number 18 was demolished first, and the whole row soon followed. The shop was a milliners owned by Sylvia Bowell, then a second hand clothing shop during the war owned by Mrs Dwyer, and finally a travel agents.

Photo c1978 showing the complete row of houses in Oxford Road, viewed from the corner of Littlehay Road towards Hendred Street. The shop on the corner was Pinkneys, originally Cullins.

And then there were none.

Although the heart was taken out of historic Cowley, the estates that had been developed with the establishment of the nearby factories were still growing. Between 1919 and 1929 only 436 private houses were built in Oxford, but between 1930 and 1937, 4336 were erected, many of these at Cowley.

Sunnyside Estate, including Fernhill, White, Wilkins, Marshall and neighbouring roads, was established between Hollow Way and what was to become the Eastern Bypass in the early 1930s. Much of the land belonged to Dr Ivy Williams and to the farming family of Whites in Temple Cowley.

Further development took place along the Oxford Road, between the Cowley Marsh and Elder Stubbs allotments. A major developer at this time was Mr F E Moss, of N Moss & Son Limited. Some of the houses were terraced three bedroomed houses and sold for £665, at a time when wages at the Pressed Steel Company were in the region of £2 10s 0d a week.

Barns Court estate, built during the 1960s, was an extension of the old Hockmore Street, on old allotment land. These houses, built by Messrs Pye Bros., and those on Sunnyside Estate, were built for private purchase.

An advert for housing on the new Florence Park Estate.

A 1940s postcard view of Lytton Road on Florence Park Estate.

Florence Park Estate mushroomed from what had been marshy land, providing new, but relatively cheap, rented accommodation for families moving into the area. Florence Park itself was built between 1933 and 1937 by Mr F E Moss, in memory of his sister, Florence, as commemorated by a plaque on the park gate. Mr Moss, himself a Welshman, responded to the demand for housing from the workers at the Morris Motors and Pressed Steel Company. Many of the new occupants of this development were immigrants from the industrial valleys of South Wales and the Yorkshire conurbations, both areas of high unemployment in the 1930s. Because of the marshy land and poor drainage the new estate suffered from floods, until a new main drain was installed at the end of Campbell Road. In the 1930s and '40s Florence Park Estate was literally thronged with young children, so much so that accommodation at the Donnington School was almost confined to the estate.

Development continues in 1955 with conversion of St Christopher's School to housing.

Similar work being carried on at Don Bosco Hall at the top of Temple Road. This building belonged to the Salesian College and was built as an assembly and functions hall. During the war years it accommodated boys from the Salesian Colleges at Chertsey and Battersea. After the war it became the College's gymnasium and the venue for boxing tournaments. The College had its own boxing team which was quite famous under trainer Father 'Killer' Jennings.

Shops and Businesses

The main shops of Cowley were concentrated in Between Towns Road, formerly known as Cowley High Street and Oxford Road. Small businesses started as a direct result of the nearby factories and to cater for the factory workers.

Bates Garage, Oxford Road. The original premises c1926.

Albert Bates lived at 95 Oxford Road, Cowley and worked at the Church Army Press. In the mid 1920s he purchased a plot of land on the corner of Edmund Road and Oxford Road from Mrs Lee, landlady of the Exeter Hall, and a garage was started in 1926. A hand operated petrol pump was installed, the first one east of Oxford.

The premises in 1930. The original building was soon replaced, with living accommodation and a tea room above. The tea room catered for the workers at the MG factory in Edmund Road, built in 1927. Bicycles became an integral part of the business, with elaborate window displays a feature. The Morris Garages can be seen on the left, at the bottom of Edmund Road. The two other shops were The Cowley Music and Wireless Salon and Reg and Freddie Law, shoe repairers.

Oxford Road during the 1950s, looking towards the Swan, showing the garage of A F Bates on the right hand side.

Shergolds in Hollow Way

Stanley Shergold left school in the late 1920s and started an apprenticeship in an ironmongers shop in Marlborough on a starting pay of five shillings a week. In 1932, just before his twenty first birthday, he visited Oxford and, through friends, found an empty unit in a row of six shops that had just been built in Hollow Way, Cowley. He took the unit at a rent of £1 a week, with an option to buy for £525 after one year. Business was brisk and he expanded into an adjoining unit and added a first floor. Amongst his customers he supplied the car factories with precision tools. At first he made deliveries in an Austin Van, but, because of his close association with Morris Motors, thought it prudent to change to a Morris Van! After the war business boomed and, from his humble beginnings in Hollow Way, he eventually became chairman of a chain of fifty shops.

Hopkins in Hollow Way, Cowley was established in 1920 as a grocers, by Mrs Eva Hopkins, to serve the local community. Claude Hopkins, her son, joined the business in the mid 1920s. His wife, Edna, started selling a selection of paints and wallpapers, from the front room of her house next door to the store. In 1946 Claude Hopkins branched out to form a separate company trading as plumbers merchants in Magdalene Road, Oxford. Claude's son, Grahame, took over this operation in 1951. In 1981 the two businesses were merged to form Hopkins of Cowley Limited. The premises in Hollow Way were sold in 1994, completely demolished, and the site developed into flats.

Chris Harper started business in the 1920s, after a spell as an insurance broker and service with the Royal Engineers. His first shop was a shed on a plot of land opposite the factory in Garsington Road. With the expansion of Morris Motors and the building of the Pressed Steel Company, he had realised the potential in the sale of bicycles for the vast numbers of workers. The 'early years were spent mending punctures for the work force and, with the thousands of bicycles required by the Cowley workers, business expanded.

Harpers in Garsinton Road.

A purpose built shop was built and he acquired the franchise with Raleigh Bikes, which assured the future prosperity of the business. In later years Harpers stocked motorcycles and acquired business links with Honda. Further expansion on the site resulted in The House of Honda which opened in 1970.

Johnson's Cafe can be seen next to Harpers. This cafe started in the early 1920s to cater for the factory workers. Today it is as popular as ever.

Johnson's Cafe, adjacent to Harpers.

Alders Newsagents — Oxford Road, this photograph, taken c1924/25, shows Frederick Alder on the right, his son Albert Alder (always knows as Nor) in the middle, with an unknown gentleman on the left.

Frederick Alder started business from his home in Crescent Road, which was turned into a small shop, selling newspapers, confectionery and tobacco. He used to take lemonade on a trolley to the cricket ground at the top of Crescent Road. He moved to a shop at the lower end of Oxford Road, near the Elder Stubbs Allotment, and eventually to a purpose built shop further up the Oxford Road, nearer The Swan.

The existing shop was originally No 60 Oxford Road, but renumbered to 126 Oxford Road. This photograph shows Dorothy Alder, wife of 'Nor', outside the shop c.1930s. Pete Alder, grandson of the founder, recently retired from the business, but the shop keeps the name of Alder.

11 Belcher Edmnd. Fred

...... here is Lytton rd ......

13 Shayler Sydney Jas
15 Thomas Iorwerth
17 Poore Chas. Jas
19 Hall Lionel G
19 Jones Mrs. M
21 Durban Ernest V. G
23 Tolputt Edwd. Finnis

OVAL (THE),
Rose Hill.
From Ashurst way.

..... here is Lenthall rd .....

OXFORD ROAD,
Cowley.

Continuation of Cowley road
to Garsington road.

South-west side.

2 Stockford Gordon
4 Sheehan Anthony W. D
6 George Mrs. Ellen, shpkpr
6 George Thos
8 George Rupert
10 McDowall Jn. M
12 Oxford & District Co-
   operative Society Ltd.
   funeral directors
12 Seall Tom Herbt

...... here is George st ......

14 Bonnet Box (Mrs. E.
   Dwyer, proprietress),
   wardrobe dlrs
16 Hengoed Philip
18 Bowell Thos. Rd
20 Browning Mrs. A
22 Harris Fredk. Mrs
24 Middleton Mrs
26 Williams Trevor
28 Dyer Mrs. A. M
30 Cullen Miss Lizzie, shop-
   keeper
30 Emanuel Archbld. W. W

..... here is Littlehay rd .....

32 Grace Fredk. shopkpr
34 White Rt. Wm
36 Payne Jsph. Benj
38 Johnson Chas. smallholdr
44 Merritt Alfd. Thos
46 Law F. W. & R. boot mkrs
48 & 50 Bates A. F. Ltd.
   cycle dlrs

...... here is Edmund rd ......

52 Ewers Jn. Arth. butcher
54 Oakley Wltr. J
56 Aries Mrs

.... here is Clive rd ....

126 Alder F. & Son, newsagts
128 Hobbs G. & C. butchers
128 Spiritualist Church
130 Home & Colonial Stores
   (H. & C. (Retail) Ltd)
132 Eden G. W. & Son,
   greengros
134 Westminster Bank Ltd.
   (D. Grammer, mngr)
136 Jubilee Lending Library
   (Ernest F. Wheeler,
   propr.),   statnrs.
   tobccnsts. & confctnrs
138 Everett Ernest Wm
138 Claydon Wltr. J. fishmgr

..... here is Havelock rd .....

140 Hills Mrs. S
140 Fenn Walter G., L.D.S.
   dental surgn
142 & 144 Oxford & District
   Co-operative   Society
   Ltd. drapers
144A, Ling Chas. Fredk
146 Scroggs Harold Edwd.
   dairyman

148 **FREEFIELDS**
   (W. H. Gatfield & F.
   Powell, proprs.),
   florists & nurserymen
148A, Davic Equipment Ltd.
   electrcl. engnrs
150 Merediths (H. J. Bryant,
   propr.), outfitters
152 Frith Mrs. Sarah, grocer
154 Moderne (Leslie Frank
   Dearlove), ladies' hair-
   dressers
   Gale   Bernard,   photo-
   grapher

... here is Cleveland drive ...

156 Webb Jn. E. butcher
158 Rose Geo. B. chemist
158 Wood Clement Jesse
160 Page Mrs
162 Allport Albt
164 Firth   Edwd.   K.   A.,
   M.B., Ch.B., M.R.C.S.,
   L.R.C.P.   physcn.   &
   surgn. (Temple cott.).
   Tel. No. Oxford 7024
   Barclays   Bank   Ltd.
   H. Hudson, manager)
   Hudson Hy. (Bank ho)
174 Chaw Harold Wm

176 Gibbons Jn. Evelyn
178 Dunford Ernest, butcher
180 Silk's Stores (Midlands)
   Ltd. grocers
182 Merediths (H. J. Bryant,
   propr.), boot dlrs
184 Beechey W. F. baby
   carriage dlr
   Cowley Workers' Social
   Club (Ernest A. How-
   kins,   sec. ;   Philip
   Grace, steward) (The
   Village ho)

..here is Between Towns rd..

Original Swan Hotel, Geo.
G. Linsdell

Roman Catholic Primary
School (Our Lady) (Sister
Charlotte, head mistress)

North-east side.

...... here is Marsh rd ....

Exeter Hall P.H. Regnld.
C. King
3 Norris Chas
5 Brooks Ernest
7 Gurden Mrs
9 Hamblin Wilfred
11 Benwell Horatio
13 Fraser Mrs. V. M. wardrobe dlr
15 Willis Mrs. E. greengro
17 Yerbury Mrs
19 Cook Geo. Victor
21 Keep Mrs. E
23 Smart Stanley
25 Franks, grocers
27 Norris Wm. B
29 Roberts Wm. Hy
31 Lee Jn
33 Lord Mrs. L
35 Posselwhite Geo. Hy
37 Clements Mrs
37 Clements Miss Julie,
   ladies' hairdrssr
   Morriss Fredk. J. decrtr.
   (workshop)
   Emmanuel Hall
39 Gibbs Fras. Alfd. David
41 Thirtle Geo
43 Davies Jas
45 Spiller Regnld. C., M.A.
   (University reader in
   mineralogy)
47 Munt Edwd
49 Short Chas. hairdrssr
49 Mitchell Chas. Edwd
51 McCarthy Mrs

Oxford Road, Cowley from Kellys Trade Directory 1949
With permission from Kellys Directories Limited

OXFORD ROAD, COWLEY.

A postcard view of Oxford Road

OXFORD ROAD—continued.
53 Hedge Rt. Chas. & Sons, carpntrs
55 Surman Mrs
57 Bartlett Fredk
59 Smith Thos
61 Yeates Cyril Jsph
63 Brandish Mrs
65 Painter Mrs. M
67 Williams Lewis
69 Keene Felix
71 Hilsdon Thos
73 Morriss Fredk. J. decrtr. (yard)
73 Read Chas. Rt

75 **RIVERS GERALD,** decorator (all types of decorating undertaken)

77 Simpson Matthew
79 Hazell Jn
81 Barney Victor Chas
83 Upstone Frank Regnld
85 Robinson Edwd. Wm
87 Aris Jsph
89 Bryan Hy. Cecil F
91 Knapp Harry
93 Wells Mrs. G.wool stores
95 Bates A. F. Ltd. radio & electrical engineers

97 Carter Mrs. Alice, shop-keeper
99 Davies Aug. G
99 Swell Frank, boot repr
    Organ E. & Son, bldrs. (yard)
101 Lee Edwd
111 Baker Arth
113 Hartley Rt
115 Hartland Harry
115 Hartland H. & Son, carpntrs
117 Cherry Mrs
119 Clark Mrs. A. M
121 Tomkins Fredk. Jn
123 Alexander Thos. Jas
125 Bishop Clifford Jas
127 King Fredk. Wm
129 Modern Press (The) (L. R. & E. Hill, proprs.), printers
129 Hill Eric Leonard B
131a. Cope Bert
131 Wise Mrs. Gladys N. refrshmnt. room
133 Roby C. J. hairdrssr
135 Allaway Herbt. Cecil
137 Alder Mrs
139 Smythe Chas. Hewit

141 Pott Gordon Wm
143 Butler Sydney
145 Bonner Mrs
149 Lee Geo
151 Ellis Frank Wm
153 Bunting Mrs
155 Walker Chas. Thos
157 Outram G. H
159 Witney Wm. Hy
161 Dartnell Chas. Edwd
163 Watson Rt. Jn
165 Jones Ernest
167 Bates Geo. Arth. tobac-conist, & post office
169 West Mrs
    Temple Cowley Congre-gational Church
...... here is Temple rd ......
    St. Luke's Church
...... here is Hollow way ......

OXPENS BYEPASS (THE),

St. Thomas'.
From Osney lane to 22 New street. St. Ebbe's.
East side.
Oxford Cattle Market
...... here is Abbey pl ......

Oxford Road, Cowley from Kellys Trade Directory 1949
With permission from Kellys Directories Limited

Oxford Road parade of shops

In 1937 a row of shops was built in the Oxford Road, near The Swan, by a Mr King from Boars Hill. The shops were for rent at £2 a week. In 1968 a compulsory purchase order was served on the properties for redevelopment; it is ironic that this site has remained derelict ever since.

Bill Beechey was born in 1908 and, after leaving the Weslyan School in Oxford, he spent three years as an office boy at John Allen & Son at Cowley. At 18 years of age he emigrated to Australia but returned when he was 22. Bill became a coach trimmer at Morris Motors Limited where he spent nine and a half years. Bill decided to enter business selling baby carriages, toys and cigarettes. Business was difficult in the late 1930's and Bill got a job as a telephonist at night, leaving his wife to run the business. Business improved after the War and Beechey's became popular with local mothers and children.

The Oxford & Cowley Ironworks. This photograph was taken in 1950 and shows the original site; in later years the factory expanded into the fields next to the Oxford Stadium, known as Johnsons' Fields, and also took over the bungalow and garden facing the Watlington Road. Note the line of poplar trees lining Sandy Lane; the solitary house is White Buffalo, still standing. The Ironworks was opened on the Watlington Road in 1935. It was started by Walter Deane, who had a ironmongery shop on the corner of Dawson Street, Cowley Road. The company is now known as Dyers (Structural Steelworks) Ltd.

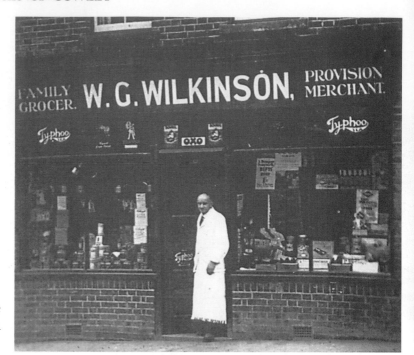

Mr Wilkinson outside his grocers shop in Crescent Road.

Sunnyside Bakery

William Payne worked with his brother-in-law, Fred Grace, in a bakery behind Honours Shop in Crescent Road. In 1932 William bought land on Sunnyside, between Marshall Road and Bleeche Place, and had a bakery built.

As well as the bakery William kept pigs and chickens. The bread delivery cart was pulled by a pony called Maggie, which was stabled on the site. William's son, Roy, helped with the delivery of the bread and later became a partner.

During the period of rationing the bakery would run out of ingredients and the local people would take in their own ingredients to be baked on the premises. At Christmas the six ovens were used to cook the turkeys, chickens and meat for the locals. The bakery finally closed in 1955 on the death of William Payne. The building can still be seen behind the warehouse that now occupies the site.

W G Powell Ltd, timber and builders merchants, the original premises in mid 1920s.

Company transport in the 1930s.

Walter Gladstone Powell was born in Birmingham in 1898, moving to Oxford in the early 1900s and settling in the Cowley Road. Walter's father, John, dealt in standing timber and, after leaving school, Walter and his brother-in-law, Arnold Lee, started in the timber trade by making sheds on the Cowley Road site. In 1923 Walter ventured into business on his own and gradually built up the successful family run timber merchants of today.

Organs, builders merchants and timber yard. The family of Albert Thomas and his wife Sarah seated in the centre, standing at the back are children Gladys, Arthur Thomas and young Bert, and seated are Jim and Annie, with young Harold in front.

In the 1870s Ephraim and David Organ came to Oxford from North Nibley in Gloucester and set up in business as carpenters and joiners in rented premises in Randolph Street, Cowley. Their brother, Albert Thomas Organ, joined them later.

The Organs owned a timber yard at Temple Road, Cowley which was eventually purchased by Albert Thomas from his brother 'Eph' and these premises became known as A T Organ & Sons. Early business at the Cowley yard consisted of tree felling, general carpentry and making firelighters. Organs Reliance Firelighters, packed in brown paper with a pink label, became known throughout the Oxford area. Later products included garden sheds, greenhouses, cages for battery hens and veneered dashboards for Morris motorcars, whose first factory in the old Military College, lay behind the timber yard.

The Factories

Morris Garages Ltd, Edmund Road

From the newspaper Jacksons Oxford Illustrated 1928:

'Remarkable Growth of the Undertaking: It is a commonly accepted truism that the obvious often escapes notice. A case in point is the remarkable growth of Morris Garages Ltd., of which Mr W R Morris is the governing director, but which is in every way distinct from the parent undertaking at Cowley. Like that, it has grown from small beginnings in a way little short of phenomenal, thanks largely to the enterprise and initiative of its general manager, Mr Cecil Kimber.

This development has now necessitated the erection of a large factory, an acre in extent, at Cowley, embodying all the necessary machinery to meet the growing demand for the 'M.G.' car, not only at home but abroad. The 'M.G.' models, with their distinctive lines and colourings, have long since established themselves in popular favour, the difficulty is to supply the increasing market as is evidenced by the fact that the company is behind with deliveries. It is hoped, however, with the general speeding up which has been brought about by centralising the many activities of the firm, to remedy this in the near future.

A visit to the new works, which are adjacent to the main road to Cowley, just beyond the City boundary, is to be recommended to all interested in car construction, for here one is able to see a super-car assembled under ideal conditions and subjected to tests which should satisfy the super-critical. In its progress through the works the familiar Morris engine is subjected to special overhaul and careful tuning to fit it for the high speeds of which the 'M.G.' car is capable, and the many improvements evolved by Mr Kimber are added. The car owner with a liking for superior coachwork, graceful lines, really efficient braking and those distinctive "gadgets" which are standard with 'M.G.' models will find himself longing to join the army of 'M.G.' enthusiasts. No car could possibly be subjected to more severe tests; speeds of 74 miles per hour were set up for the benefit of those who were shown over the works on Thursday afternoon, after Mr Kimber had presided at a delightfully informal luncheon party held at the Clarendon Hotel. Among those who came to "See things for themselves" were members of the directorates of Morris Motors Ltd and the Pressed Steel Company, and congratulations were showered upon Mr Kimber on the capital lay-out of the works and the expansion of the business'. The 'M.G.' Factory in Edmund Road, Cowley was subsequently moved to Abingdon in 1929. '

A chassis with a loaded test body goes out on a road test.

The Running-in Bay, where chassis are tested for three days, the rear wheels resting on rollers with air fans attached. On the first day they are run at an engine speed of 1000 rpm on low gear, the second day at 1250 rpm on second gear and the third day at 1500 rpm on top gear.

The First Bay, where the engines are taken down, the valve parts are ground and polished, the bearings bedded in, stronger valve springs fitted etc.

MG cars on a test run from the factory in Edmund Road

Pressed Steel Fisher

Extract from an in-house publication of 1950

'At the far end of the suburb of Cowley is the huge plant of Pressed Steel Company Limited, and there the tradition of craftsmanship, and knowledge of engineering techniques, are held in high esteem and have so been since its inauguration in 1926. In result, from a simple origin the Company has risen to greatness in the short space of 24 years.

At the inception of the Company in 1926 the plant occupied a total floor area of 533,050 square feet. The concern thus constituted, even at that time, a manufacturing organisation of some standing, with a productive area equal to that of many organisations of repute. In 1950, however, the process of expansion had continued to such an extent that the total floor space amounted to more than two and a quarter million square feet. There were certain years in which growth was on a particularly large scale – in 1938 an area equivalent to Lord's Cricket Ground was added – but it is interesting to note that the total increase in factory area did not result from a few extensions of this magnitude. On the contrary a steady process of expansion has been maintained in almost unbroken annual sequence, for of the past 24 years there have been very few which have not seen an increase in the total of productive floor space.

During the first eight years, expansion, although consistent, was not spectacular, but at the end of the next three years the original figure of some half a million square feet had been doubled and thus in 1937 more than one million square feet of floor space were devoted to the important task of manufacturing car bodies and refrigerators. Although this "doubling up" from half a million to one million square feet was in itself no light achievement, it was surpassed when the procedure was repeated and the one million subsequently became more than two million in the comparatively short space of 13 years.

In 1936 a new block was added to house the Management and Main Office staff, followed by a large Canteen for the staff and works personnel. A new, well-equipped Hospital was erected in 1937 whilst the Press Shop contained in the structure known as 'R' building was added in 1938. It is almost 500 feet long – approximately the length of St Paul's Cathedral – and 60 feet wide and contains some 80 power presses with pressures up to 900 tons. Although this building is a large one, it is outstripped by the main Press Shop, which is actually longer than the Houses of Parliament, and is the largest Press Shop in Europe. 'S' building with its Press Shop, completed early in the war, was responsible for aircraft sub-assemblies of many kinds.

In 1941 a new factory was erected to serve wartime production purposes, but after the conclusion of hostilities this was converted for the manufacture of domestic refrigerators. A Laboratory block equipped with the most up-to-date scientific research instruments was also built in 1941. The story of expansion through the years is fittingly brought up to date – although not, it is certain to final conclusion – by mention of a new building completed in 1950 to house under one roof all members of the Engineering Department.

Today the total owned by the Company is 130 acres, which is almost half the size of London's Hyde Park, and within its boundaries more than 9,000 persons are employed.'

Assembly Line in 1940s

In 1932 the manufacture of domestic refrigerators was commenced and the name of 'Prestcold' was registered, soon to become a household name for fridges and washing machines.

Other miscellaneous products included the famous 'Mobo' steel horse

Nearly 50 special buses and coaches are required each day to transport employees to and from the Works, forming, as they roll along in apparently endless process, Pressed Steel Company's own 'Parade of Transport'.

Memories of Pressed Steel ...

'I started work at the Pressed Steel factory at Cowley in 1934. I remember it was on St Giles's Fair day, which is always held in Oxford in early September. My wages then was roughly a shilling an hour. I was put on 'trucking', that's moving big trucks of car parts about from one part of the factory to another so that they could be assembled.

Of course I am talking about a time of mass unemployment. It was terrible to see the queues of men, hundreds of them waiting outside the factory gates at six o'clock in the morning, just in case a few were needed. The foreman would go outside to the queue and shout "All right, let's have the first three men". And that was it — the other poor devils, some with tears in their eyes, turned and walked away and then went off somewhere else to try their luck. Mind you, half the time we was only working for two days a week and sometimes it was just for two hours a day, on piecework of course, so you was only paid for what you done. When there was no work there was nothing else for it but to get on your bike and come home.' (Chatto Windus).

The tide begins to flow – the first of the 9,000

Cyclists pour out of the factory in the 1940s.

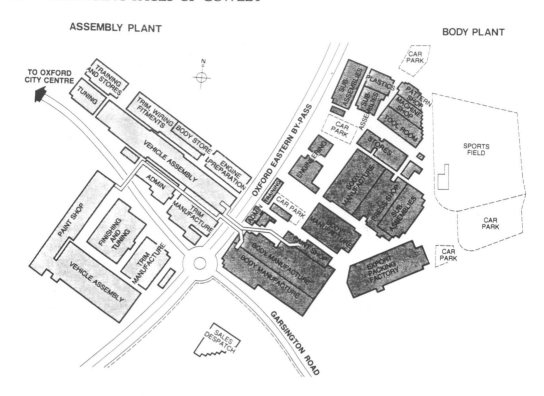

Plan of Cowley manufacturing complex.

An early Morris Motors outing. Mr Lewis Cartwright, wearing flat cap on extreme right of photograph, was a school friend of William Morris and, when Lewis was laid off at Birkenhead, he telegraphed to Morris 'have you got a job for me?' Back came the reply — 'can you start on Monday?'

Impressive display of Bullnose Morris cars in 1926

Early production line in the trimming department, 1926.

Morris's had their own fire service. This photo of 1929 shows a fire tender in Hollow Way (OPA)

Nuffield Exports on the airfield at Lydde, Kent

Aerial view taken before 1925. This shows the extent of the works at that time, and the Cowley Industrial School – the Poplars – in the background, and what was to become the site of the Pressed Steel Company. In the foreground are the cottages that occupied the site of what is now St. Luke's Church.

Morris Cowley station opened at the end of 1928. Mr Aherne was appointed Station Master and remained at Cowley until the closure of the station in 1965.

The Goods Shed at Morris Cowley Station in 1929.

On 24 October 1864 the Wycombe Railway Company opened its Oxford-Cowley-Thame line which was taken over by the Great Western Railway some six years later. The line was single broad gauge and ran four trains each way on weekdays and two on Sundays, stopping at Garsington Halt, on the Garsington Road, about one mile from Cowley. With the arrival of the motor industry the railway played a greater part in Cowley life and when the Pressed Steel Company was built in 1926 the close proximity of the railway was put to good use.

Aerial view of Morris Exports in 1934.

A Metro Tank at Morris Cowley station

Showing the close proximity of the rail lines to the factory. The company had track laid around the factory and ran their own engines on site for many years, but the engines were not allowed on the main line. Cowley maintains a freight depot and cars are still transported by rail; the factory lines, however, have ceased to exist.

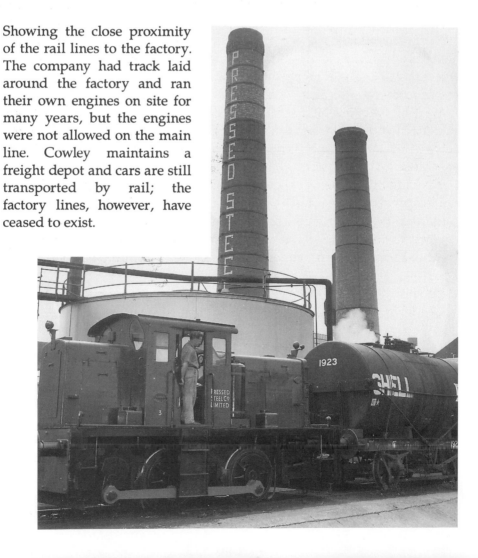

Nuffield Press

The Nuffield Press was founded in 1925 as Morris-Oxford Press Limited. At that time the Cowley factory was producing nearly 60,000 cars a year, and William Morris was expanding rapidly. Morris decided to produce his own motoring magazine, specifically for owners of Morris vehicles — the 'Morris Owner'.

A journalist, Miles Thomas, later to become Lord Thomas, was given the task of setting up the in-house printing department with Mr C A Coates as General Manager. Premises in Morris's original old factory were vacated and the company was established, with a collection of small letterpress machines. While the Morris-Oxford Press was essentially an in-house operation, external work was undertaken from the beginning. The 'Morris-Owner' proved a large and enduring success with the print order rising to about 20,000 per issue. By 1935 the Press employed 50 people.

During the Second World War the Press was given the highly confidential task of printing production documents to enable Spitfire aircraft to be manufactured, and because of the national defence implications of this and other work, including production of tank manuals, the premises were designated as an official security zone. On 4 September 1942, following Morris becoming Viscount Nuffield, the company name was changed to The Nuffield Press Limited.

As car manufacture became concentrated on the other side of Hollow Way, space became available and the Nuffield Press staked its claim. The 'Morris Owner' was succeeded by a similar magazine for Morris customers called 'New Outlook' which was followed by 'Motoring'. By 1950 twelve and a half million copies of these magazines alone had been printed by the Press. The turning point, technically, came in 1955 when a large lithopress was acquired. This was a two-colour press which could be expanded to produce three and four colour works. Nuffield Press kept pace with technology and, while geographically it remained exactly in the same place it was founded, the business had come a long way from the Morris in-house printing department to become a major organisation meeting the printing needs of a wide range of customers.

The company changed hands several times and has now vacated the premises, thus severing Cowley's last industrial links with William Morris.

The history of the Nuffield Press buildings

The original buildings were founded as Cowley College in 1841. The 17th century Manor House, demolished in 1957, was extended and became the main building of this College. A chapel was added in 1870 and, by 1876, the college was known as Hurst's Grammar School and included a large stone house built on the corner of Oxford Road and Hollow Way. The upper rooms were dormitories, the lower ones were schoolrooms built to the very latest design, including an early form of central heating. Despite its initial success, the school closed during the early 1870s.

The Oxford Military College Limited acquired the buildings from Robert Hurman, second and last headmaster of Hurst's Grammar School and the new Military College opened in September 1876. The premises were far from perfect and the buildings were further extended by the building of two three-storey wings to the east and south by the architect Thomas Graham Jackson. An Oxford architect, H G W Drinkwater, was commissioned to design a swimming bath and a science laboratory. The Military College survived until bankruptcy forced its closure in 1896.

The premises were acquired by William Morris in 1912 and the East Wing was converted to accommodate the factory. Morris's own office was established on the first floor of the stone school house overlooking the Oxford Road.

A sketch of the existing buildings and the proposed extensions 1877. The extensions were never completed.

A riding squad inside the courtyard.

Group of Corporals in 1883. Back row: L C F Tufnell, R F G Faussett, R de C Boyd, E F Buttanshaw, E C M Parry, G Bidie, T B Dixon, A E Buckle, H E MacDonnell. Front row: C Ashburnham, F H Hotham, L T C Twyford, G L Hibbert, Hon H D Napier, F C Laing. Seated on ground: R F Knollys, J L Sinclair.

The swimming pool for the Military Cadets, later used by Morris Motors and local schools

Morris Motors cars in Hollow Way, pre 1925.

The East Wing of the buildings facing Hollow Way.

The Nuffield Press buildings facing The Swan. The three-storey extension, protruding from the original Military College building, was built in 1931.

The 'Morris Owner' — the reason for the establishment of the 'in-house' printing company. This issue, Volume II number 5, is dated July 1925 and is priced at 4d.

Mr W Haines, Senior Operator, at work on a Monotype Keyboard in 1938. Above the keyboard a roll of paper was suspended and, as each key was depressed, the paper was perforated. This perforated record, when transferred to the casting machine, automatically controlled the casting of the type. The keyboard was powered by compressed air, some operators could achieve more than 10,000 key stokes per hour.

Mr R J Brown and Mr A C Ayres making-up pages for 'The Mirror', the in-house magazine in 1938.

The Composing Room 1943. Centre is Cyril King with Walter Horne 3rd from the left.

One of the two Composing Rooms in 1938. Activities included typesetting, correcting and proofing, making-up into pages and imposing, i.e. the arrangement of the pages of type and blocks in the correct position so that when the sheet is printed and folded the printed pages appear in the correct sequence. The wooden roof beams were needed to support the weight of the binding department on the floor above.

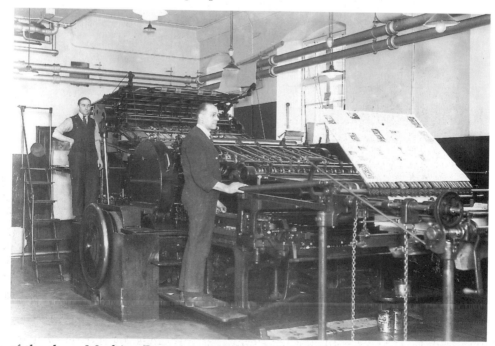

One of the three Machine Rooms in 1938. Mr. W. Ansell on duty, with assistance from Mr. F. Loveridge at the back.

The Binding Department, c1948, with Frank Eltome operating the folding machine which automatically produced over 3000 folded sheets per hour.

A photograph of 1938 showing the feeder-stitcher machines, by means of which the sheets and cover were wire stitched at a rate of over 3000 complete magazines per hour. Left to right: Edna Hartley, Dot Brown, Gladys Johnson, -?-.

A general view of the Binding Department c1948. Left to right: Ken Broster, -?-, -?-, Mrs Gobey, Margaret Brookes, -?-, June Franklin, Amy Titterton, Connie Walker (at back) others unknown.

Nearing the end of the line in 1938. Ralph Hanger trimming the magazine at the guillotines, ready for counting and dispatching.

Recreation

The Cowley Workers Social Club, it is said, was formed by a group of people who left the Cowley Conservative Club to form a new club for working men. These founders were Harold Turner, a carrier who became the Club's first president, Joe Pocock, Harry Pruce, Trevor Jones, Bill Wilkinson, H R Smith and Claude Roche. They met in the Village House, on the corner of Oxford Road and Between Towns Road, where the Club was formed on 15 April 1929, opening on 31 May 1929. The Cowley Workers Social Club moved to new £140,000 premises in Between Towns Road in 1970. The Barns Road Residents' Association, later to become the Cowley Community Association, was founded in 1945.

Cowley Workers Photograph — Pontoon outing 1950s. Left to right back row: Jack Whittaker, Arthur Knight, Darkie ?, Davy McBlain, -?-, Len Reynolds, -?-, Vic Perry, Guy Baker, Ras Chapman, Jed Sillman, Arthur Kingston, Aubrey Godfrey, (driver unknown), Ray Berry, Henry Knowles, Ray Band, Ron Godfrey, Harry Butcher, Ted Knowles, -?-, Stan ?, John Warland, Eddie Lockey. Front row: Eric Johnson, Monty Greenaway, Syd Newbold, Freddie Guilders, Stan Norton, Ralphy Robson, Pat Tuttle, Windsor Lewis, -?-.

The Cowley Male Voice Choir, shown here in 1933

Following the First World War, Britain suffered the worst depression since the Industrial Revolution. Unemployment was rife and nowhere was the anguish and despair more keenly felt than in the mining valleys of South Wales. The General Strike of 1926 lasted nine days; the miners' strike of the same year lasted nine months. By 1930 unemployment in South Wales reached a staggering 33% Against this background of despondency and despair young men had two choices — to join the dole queue, or leave home and look for work elsewhere. Many emigrated to various parts of the British Empire others to the larger English cities where new industries were beginning to flourish.

Cowley was expanding rapidly and the Pressed Steel Company, in particular, was looking for unskilled and semi-skilled workers. Many Welshmen made that long journey to Cowley; some walked, some cycled, sleeping rough or in work houses and doss houses en route. Often the first port of call was the Village House, a lodging house which flourished on the corner of Between Towns Road, opposite the Swan. There they heard news of relatives and friends who had preceded them on the great trek. Some of these men met up in local pubs and would begin to sing the melodies of their childhood. Other Welshmen heard of this and soon joined in: thus the Party was born in 1928 in the Cape of Good Hope on the Plain near Oxford.

An Alan Course cartoon, courtesy of *The Oxford Mail*

Haydn Evans

Haydn came to Oxford from Merthyr Tydfil in 1933 at the age of 22. He worked at the Pressed Steel factory for 41 years. Haydn has performed in more than 600 concerts with the choir, many of them as a solo performer. He is President of the Choir.

The Cowley Congregational Church, led by their minister, the Reverend Whatley White, allowed the choir to rehearse on Church premises. Later premises included St Christopher's School in Cowley. Alderman Fred Moss, a native of Merthyr Tydfil, gave them encouragement and financial support, eventually becoming President. In 1931 The Party changed its name to Oxford Welsh Prize Glee Singers; the 'Prize' being dropped soon after, and it has remained the Oxford Welsh Glee Singers ever since. Names from those early attendance registers include Tom Bevan, Haydn Evans, Morgan Williams, Mel Davis, Tom Jones, Billo Roberts, Howell Thomas, Gwyn Lloyd, Wynn Jones and Willie Davies, who was conductor for fourteen years until his resignation in 1950.

The Party moved to the newly built Cowley Community Centre in 1965, where they still rehearse regularly every Friday night.

The Women's Fellowship was a church group, run by Sister Cain. This photograph was taken during the 1930s outside St James's Parish Hall.

The Ancient Order of Britons outside the Carpenters Arms in the 1920s

The first Inter-Track Race at Oxford against Wembley in 1940. Left to right: Mr C J V Bellamy, Mayor of Oxford 1939-40, F Wise, J P Young, Mrs Bellamy, Bill Davies, Miss Rice, Bill Higgins, Mr. Blanch (veterinary surgeon), Miss Wakelin, Miss Gomershall, Percy East, Miss Fright, Jim Tanner.

'The correct uniform for a kennel lad was tight black boots with riding breeches and yellow polo neck shirts for men, white shirt and tie with a riding cap for girls. Wages for a kennel lad was £1 for a seven day week.'

Oxford Stadium was opened on 31 March 1939 by Lord Denham. Winners at that first greyhound meeting were: Hunting Snipe, No Race, Wax End, Diamond Glory, Mickie Jay, Second Advent, Hunting Castle and Candys Ataxy. Trainers in those early days were Davies, Preston, Higgins, McMaster and Mullins. Greyhound meetings were held on Tuesdays and Fridays.

At the outbreak of the war racing was stopped as floodlights could not be used, then restarted in March 1940 for one meeting a week on Saturday afternoons or Friday evenings in summer time. During the war the kennel lads and staff formed a Local Defence Volunteers unit with *'one rifle, five bullets and one pair of binoculars'*.

Speedway started at the Stadium on Saturday evenings. A popular rider in 1939 was Danny Lee, a Byfleet boy, who lodged locally for a time.

A speedway meeting in late 1938. Back row includes: Bob Jones, Ron Wilkins, R G F Faulkner, Bill Simms, Jim Boyd, Jeff Harling, Arthur Flack, Ted Mander, Les Sammons, Tommy Hayhow, Pip Barrett, Ginger Welch, Arthur Peck. Front row includes: George Bason, Bert Waller, Fred Davies, Bill Newell, Buster Yeomons, Roy Duke, Arthur Sweby, Pete Minns.

The Morris Motor Band was formed in 1924 and sponsored by William Morris, later Lord Nuffield. Harry Mortimer, their musical director for over thirty years, was the driving force behind the band's successes. The band became extremely well known throughout the country, touring abroad and often playing to audiences of 10,000. Vacancies were advertised in the band magazine and, as band members had to work at the Morris Motors factory, successful musical applicants could be assured of a job.

Morris Motors Band c1948, outside the Chapel of the former Military College (Nuffield Press) in Oxford Road, Cowley. Back row left to right: G V Brooks, B Griffin, L Randall, D Zolinson, -?-. 4th row: G Weeks, -?-, -?-, M Merrilees, 3rd row: J Alder, C Jones, T F Morcombe, -?-, E Jones, -?-. 2nd row: -?-, R Sharpe, -?-, -?-, P Mew, -?-. Front row: -?-, C Maycock, L Harding, P Sprules, -?-, -?-

The Blue Star Players

RHYTHM SECTION

VOCAL TRIO

BRASS SECTION

SAX SECTION

'On behalf of the Club may I express my appreciation of the way your band contributed to our very successful evening, which was thoroughly enjoyed by everybody.' A W H B King, Bedford House Old Boys' Club, Oxford

The Blue Star Players were formed, in June 1932, by Stan Rogers, who was born in St Ebbes in 1905, from 'the best players from the various groups'. They played at the Morris Motors Clubhouse and in St James Parish Hall, where they attracted huge crowds during the 1930s and '40s. The original line up was Leslie Hewson (alto sax), Bill Franklin (alto sax), Bill Enoch (tenor sax), Wilf Foreman (trumpet), Lionel Abbott (bass), Bert Haithwaite (piano), Ted Baker (drums) and Stan Rogers (banjo and guitar). Les Windscheffel lived in Cowley and joined the Band a few months after it was formed, as replacement for Lionel Abbott. The Band won many contests and continued to do so right up to the 1950s, when the arrival of the teenage pop singers completely changed the music scene.

Members of the Morris Motors Motor Cycle Club c1920: Ernest Allen on the left of picture.

Golf on Cowley Marsh: Terry Exler winning the Shield.

Tennis on Cowley Marsh: Left to right: George Chapman, Les Buckingham, Pete Oakley. Standing: Frank Hilsdon, Fred Exler.

An early scout camp 1910 at Brasenose Woods, near Cowley. Standing left to right: F Morgan, W Mullard, Patrol leader Herbert, Beesley. Sitting: Humphries, Scoutmaster Bren, A Wyatt, C Wyatt, Farnell and Farnell

The Society of Scouts' Friends was formed in 1909 to collect funds to assist very poor boys to attend camp, however boys were 'always expected to pay something'. Camps used to be held under canvass in August, sometimes by the river where the Scouts could bathe, swim and boat, sometimes in nearby woods. This photograph shows an early Summer Camp of 1910.

When Baden Powell retired from the Army he took a keen interest in Youth Movements, particularly the Boys Brigade. He was asked by Sir William Smith, the founder of the Boys Brigade, to adapt his book 'Aids to Scouting' as a training manual for the Brigade and the book was to be called 'Scouting for Boys'. The book was finished in 1908 and published in twelve fortnightly parts price 4d (under 2p) each. Because they were so cheap boys from all types of families were able to buy them and these boys formed themselves in patrols and started Scouting. After a time it was recognised that Scouting was getting out of hand, with boys lighting fires in the parks, chopping down trees and causing damage everywhere. It was suggested that as Baden Powell had 'caused' Scouting by publishing his book, he should take a hand at controlling it — and so organised Scouting started.

41st Oxford Scouts 1933

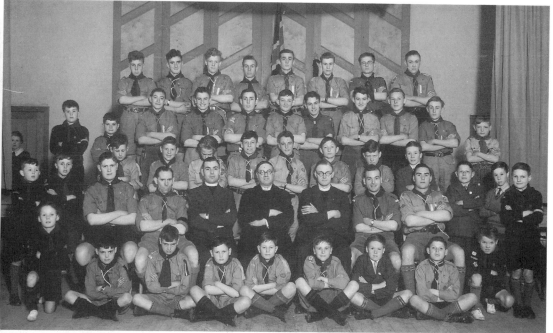

The 41st Oxford Cub Scouts (Cowley St James) c1936. Left to right back row: unknown, unknown, J Welch, K Higgins, R Johnson, unknown, unknown, D Childs. 2nd row: unknown, unknown, I Venn, D Hill, unknown, P Knights, unknown, unknown, unknown, Johnson. 3rd row: first five unknown, M Underwood, J Jarvis, unknown, unknown, B Baxter, W Knights. 4th row: first three unknown, Mr Lafford Scout Master, Fr Lewis, Fr Maurice Beauchamp, Fr Alec Whye, G Clark, unknown, unknown, A Baxter, unknown. Front row: 3rd from right R Baxter.

Programme

'THE CABIN BOY.'

A Play by the 41st Oxford Wolf Cubs.

Cabin Boy .... R. Drake
Captain .... A. Lodge
Dancers .... G. and R. Posselwhite
              Tony Webb, and Billy
              Knights
Sailors .... Rest of Cub Pack

'DICK WHITTINGTON.'

By E. Stuart Monro.

CHARACTERS IN ORDER OF APPEARANCE.

Idle Jack .... D. Hill
Village Maiden .... J. Crawford
Ursula .... S. Browning
R. Whittington .... J. Welch
Thomas the Cat .... J. Pether
Alderman Fitzwarren ...... K. Higgins
Mrs. Fitzwarren .... J. Mullard
Manservant .... K. Exler
Alice Fitzwarren .... D. Lafford

Steward .... J. Johnson
Captain Main-Brace .... G. Howitt
Sultan of Morocco .... R. Johnson
Sultan's Bodyguard
        A. Benford, P. Hull, and N. Wicks
Slave .... P. Knights
King Rat .... M. Underwood
Rat .... R. Kirtland
Chorus—Choir of St. James' Hall, Cowley.

Act. I. Scene I. Highgate Hill.
         Scene II. Alderman Fitzwarren's Count-
                       ing House.
Act. II. Scene I. The Landing Stage.
          Scene II. The S.S. 'Saucy Kipper.'
          Scene III. Shores of Morocco.
Act. III. Scene I. Sultan's Palace.
           Scene II. Rat Chamber.
           Scene III. Sultan's Palace.
Act. IV. Scene I. The Guildhall, London.

PIANIST: MISS CHILD.
ELECTRICIAN: E. VENN.

The 41st Oxford Wolf Cubs (Cowley St James) regularly produced a Gang Show or pantomime. The Grand Pantomime of 1935 was 'Dick Whittington' and 'The Cabin Boy'.

Believed to be the production of 'Cinderella' in 1933, including I Venn, D Hill, J Welch, K Higgins, R Johnson, P Knights, W Knights, R Kirtland, M Blackburn.

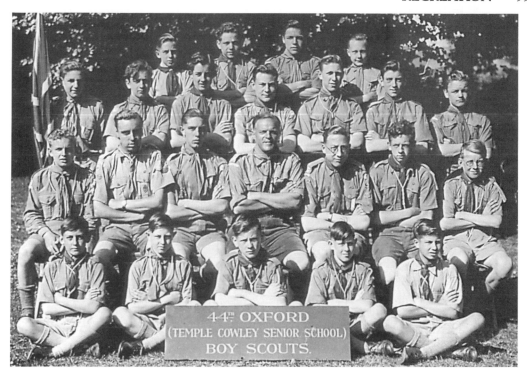

The 44th Oxford (Temple Cowley Senior School) Boy Scouts c1947. Back row left to right: Harvey Harries, Ray Holmes, David Munday, Gerald Silman. 3rd row: John Bennett, Robert Burgess, Cyril Band, Peter Swift, Arthur Brooks, Alan Wilkinson, Roy Davies. 2nd row: Peter Willet, Fred Hinton, Fred Gunn, Herman Munday, Ken Blaby, Ronald Miles, Arthur Melson. Front row: Roy Bradbury, Roy Massingham, Peter Nelmes, John Massingham, Richard Molyneux.

The 1st Cowley Guides 1936. This group were based at the Poplars, the Cowley Industrial School. Miss Haynes was the Captain, (with permission of the County Guides Executive).

The 3rd Cowley Brownies c1955 belonging to the Congregational Church in Temple Road.

The 4th Cowley Brownies in the early 1940s, practising their semaphore, skipping and ball games, near the hut behind St Francis's church in Hollow Way, (with permission of the County Guides Executive).

Scouts belonging to the Congregational Church in Temple Road in the 1950s

Health and Religion

Exterior, Convalescent Home.

The house called Sunnyside in Hollow Way, former home of Miss Ivy Williams, was opened as a convalescent home for twelve women and eight children in 1921. It was presented to the Radcliffe Infirmary by Dr Ivy Williams, together with fifty acres of land. The home was in use until 1930, when the estate was sold and part of the proceeds used to build a thirty bed convalescent hospital on the Manor House estate in Headington, on the site of the present John Radcliffe. The new building was also called Sunnyside.

Dr Ivy Williams

Oxford Times Friday 25 February 1966: *Death of Dr Ivy Williams at age of 88. Dr Ivy Williams the first woman to be called to the English Bar, died at her home in Staverton Road, Oxford on Friday after a long illness. She was 88. Dr Williams, an honourary fellow and former tutor of St Anne's College, Oxford, was called to the English Bar in May 1922, six months after Ulster-Coun. Miss Frances Kyle was called to the Irish Bar. Mrs Helena Normanton, whom some regard as the pioneer English woman barrister, was called the following November. Dr Williams earned her priority by gaining a Certificate of Honour at the Final Bar Examination. Mrs Normanton was called with other women at the regular time. Dr Williams gained her MA in 1920 and her doctorate in Civil Law three years later, both at St Anne's.*

Ivy Williams inherited property and land in Cowley from her father St Swithin Williams. During the early part of this century the family lived at 12 King Edward Street, where St Swithin practised as a solicitor and Winter Williams as a barrister-at-law. The family later lived in a large property in Hollow Way and were influential in Cowley affairs.

John Bunyan Baptist Church, Crowell Road

Stone Laying Ceremony for the main hall, 1st June 1940. The original small hall is on the left.

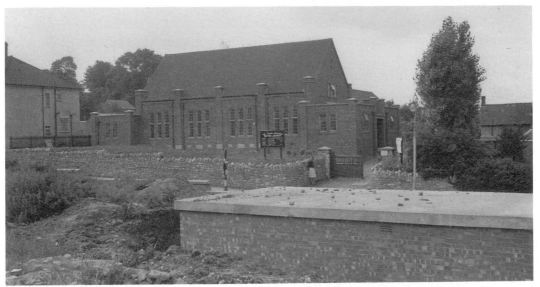

The finished main hall, June 1941, from Crowell Road, complete with the nearest air-raid shelter, now the site of Templars Square.

In the autumn of 1938 work began on the site of the new John Bunyan Baptist Church. Six months later, on 20 April 1939, the first services of worship were held in the small hall. The Rev H J White, Minister of New Road Baptist Church, was instrumental in making this happen. He was convinced that Cowley, with its rapidly expanding population, would benefit from the establishment of this church. The first Minister appointed was the Rev David Rigden Green, who *'began his ministry the day and the hour when Mr Neville Chamberlain broadcast the news at 11 a.m. on Sunday 3 September 1939, "We are at war with Germany".'*

The laying of the foundation stone at the Primitive Methodist Chapel at 39b Oxford Road, Cowley in 1903. This was called the 'Tin Tabernacle'.

The house in the background is the funeral home at 12 Oxford Road operated by Eli Smart. The Smart family were members of the Primitive Methodist Chapel in Pembroke Street (now Rectory Road) and it has been suggested that Eli may have donated the land for the building of this chapel.

The Cowley Temple of Christ: members of this Church met in the Cowley Community Centre for thirteen years, from 1956 until 1969, when the old Methodist Chapel, known as the 'Tin Tabernacle', was purchased for £2,500 and restored as a Christian Spiritualist Church.

The amalgamation of the three Spiritualist Churches in Oxford — Alma Hall Spiritualists' National Union Church, Headington Greater World Christian Spiritualist Church and the Cowley Temple of Christ Greater World Christian Spiritualist Church took place on 9 September 1968, so forming the Oxford Spiritualist Church. The founder president of the church was Mr Percy Wilson, a leading member of the Spiritualist Movement.

SECTION NINE

Sports

Concerning Cowley
Written by Thomas Preston   Sung by Percy Bell

(To the tune of *Little Brown Jug*)

The people of London, that great city,
Are still inquiring who is this Cowley,
Not far from Oxford, reached by 'bus,
Yet it is causing a mighty fuss.

Chorus
   Ha-ha-ha, he-he-he,
   Who-ev-er is this Cowley?
   Ha-ha-ha, he-he-he,
   Who-ev-er is this Cowley?

It had been rumoured they would come a cropper,
And never reach the competition proper,
But the captain of the team kept his men in bounds,
And are playing Civil Service in the first round.

Last year it seemed, they could not be beaten,
Until they came against Windsor and Eton,
They took their loss bravely, but hopes ran high
For another point better in the bye-and-bye.

From the centre forward, to Battesby
They play the game to a nice-o-ty,
Passing to each other like the proper thing,
Never forgetting the players on the wing.

To the Club Guy Sturgess is a great asset,
And his brother George, when he gets set,
Also the centre forward, good Len Rogers,
The three put together are mighty dodgers.

The two brothers Bennett, George and Bill,
You would have a job, their place to fill,
Ernie Martin, who is second to none,
Plays the game soundly, till it is won.

You have a back in George Buckingham,
Playing the game as a gentleman,
The centre half, good old Jack King,
Gives the ball a mighty sting.

The outside left, as a rule,
Is a gentleman by the name of Jewell,
Who plays as well as ever he can
And we have another in Bowerman.

Good old Didley we must not miss,
He's too good to be left out of this,
And the man who thinks of everyone,
Is good old Charlie Bevercombe.

Cowley are in the Oxfordshire
Senior League, with nothing to fear,
They are on the top at the present,
And to remain there is their intent.

Now we also have they who guide the team aright,
Who always meet on a Monday night,
Sitting round the table with ink and pen,
That's your fine Committee Men!

Now Cowley supporters are the sort
Of people who like fine sport,
They follow them through the seasons play.
Whether the match is Home or Away.

The Cowley Football Club 1919/20. Winners of the County Junior Shield and City League Division and Finalists County Charity Cup.

Back row left to right: Major G W G Allen, A Rogers, W Baker, L Rogers, W Bennett, G Buckingham, G Noke, W Barrett, Capt J J C Allen. Front row: E Allen, G Sturges, Guy Sturges (Capt), J Allen, Esq O.B.E. (President), C H Bevercombe (Hon. Sec and Treasurer), J Greenaway, C Matthews. In front: C Smith, H Blackwell.

The Sunnyside Football stand in Hollow Way, newly constructed in 1928 to accommodate 300 people.

Cowley Football team in 1905

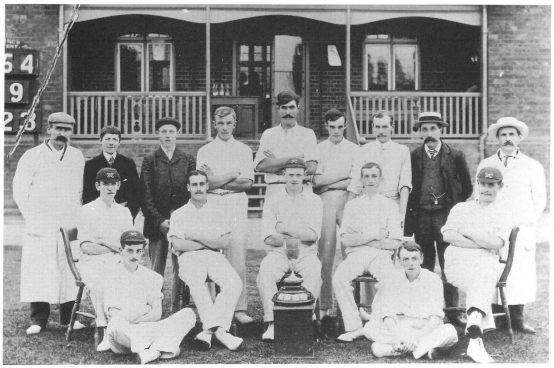

Cowley Cricket Club 2nd XI 1906 Winners of the Telegraph Cup. Left to right back row: F Bryan (umpire), F Harvey (scorer), W Rogers, J Buckingham, J Hilsdon, G Denson, G Cooper, W Wale (Sec. of Competition), J Tanner (umpire). Middle row: W Lee, C Pearson, P Sanders (Capt.), F Godfrey, A Morgan. Seated: C Grace, A Godfrey.

Church Army Press Cricket Club 1931, winners of the Airey Challenge Cup. Left to right back row: J Gurden, B R Harris, S G Windscheffel, A Windscheffel, S Burden, P Bell (scorer). Front row left to right: P T Hickman, T Maylon (Capt.), Mr R C Kent (President), J H G Hall (Hon Sec), W J Greenaway. Seated on floor: R J Goodey, J Cockram.

A local football team who played on Cowley Marsh seen here in c1930. Left to right back row: Bill Currill, Reg Bradbury, -?-. 2nd row: Les Windscheffel, -?-, Bert Moss, Archie Curry. Front row: 2nd left Bert Davis. The team were known as 'The Marsh Frogs' — a name given to anyone who had ever fallen into the Marsh brook.

A Cowley team from Florence Park, Athletico Florentina, were founder members of the Sunday League. Seen here in 1967. Left to right back row: E Sherman (Manager), D Hawkes, J Gomley, B Weston (Capt), T Cross, D Edwards, G Thompson, R Bowers. Front: B Harris, T Jones, P Kenny, G Hawkins, G Slade.

Morris Motors team in 1964. Left to right back row: B Morris, B Weston (Capt), E Griffiths, N Wastie, P Wooley, P Drake, D Hackett. Front row: T Renshaw, G Hawkins, G Wakefield, R Caffel, A Hellyer.

The British Motor Corporation: Mezz-Floor Winners of the Inter-Departmental Cricket Competition in 1968. Left to right back row: P Cox, A Richardson, L Watts, B Weston, B Boffin, T Jennings. Front row: N Brown, K Parsler, R Henwood (Capt), J Clinkard, C Bailey.

Cowley Boys Club, *a tribute to Ted Wheelock*

Cowley Boys Under 14 team 1949/50. Winners of the Cup and League. Left to right back row: Jack Lewis, Terry Foster, Michael Foster. Sitting: Ken Harris, Alan Wilmer, Trevor Lewis, John Prime, Ted Hudman, N Thomas, E Farr.

In 1947 a group of boys aged from 12 to 20, from Clive Road, George Street (now Hendred Street) and Shelley Road formed teams and played football on Cowley Marsh. They decided they would like to go competitive and, in 1948, formed a team called the Cowley Colts Football Club. The best of each team formed the side and the captain and vice captain of each team became the management committee. It was run entirely by the boys themselves. They approached the National Association of Boys Clubs for acceptance into the local leagues but their application was rejected on the grounds that they were a football club and not a Boys Club. A Boys Club had to have a headquarters, an adult management committee and a full range of activities, such as art, debating, drama etc.

Ted Wheelock, together with some parents, decided late in 1948 to set up a Boys Club. They gained the use of a hut behind the Carpenters Arms in Hockmore Street and leafleted the area. On the first evening 300 boys turned up; it was obvious there was a need for a Boys Club in Cowley. They could not cope with these numbers and the newly formed Boys Club was limited to the age range 15 to 18. Two football teams were formed, an under 16 and an under 18 side, boxing was introduced and the boys put on their first play. After two years the Club had outgrown the hut and the National Association of Boys Clubs was approached for help with premises, but none were available.

Left to right back row: Aubrey Harris (AAA starter), Ted Wheelock (leader), Mr Brookes, Mr McDowell. 2nd row: Neil Brooks, Ian McDowell, Ted Hudman, Ken Harris, John Robinson. Front row: Alan Pickford, Duncan McKenzie, Francis Parsons, Jack Woods, Jones, Peter Selwood, Jones. Early 1950s.

Cowley Boys Club Athletics team early 1950s. Left to right back row: Ted Wheelock, Lewis Gammon, John Stone, Ted Hudman, -?-, Paul Rutter, Ken Bradbury, Ken Harris, Bert Mills, Mr Brookes. Front row: Clive Jones, Alan Pickford, Stuart Grainger, Barrett, Doug Goody, Ron Dodds, Duncan McKenzie, Mick Lewin.

Cowley Boys Under 16s Football team with Rose Hill Boys c1953. Left to right back row: Mr Apsley, John Davis, Clive North, Ray Houghton, Dave Mills, Alan Richardson, Mick Honey, Terry Richards, Jim Dodds, Tom Harris, Norman Thomas, Ben Langsbury, 'Truc' Carter, K Rees(?), Alan Wilmer. In front: Colin Jackson, Eric Farr, Rick Newman, Nobby Brown, Hugh Allen, Vic Parsons(?), Keith Phelps, Roland White, Don Stewart.

In 1950, Mr King, the headmaster at Temple Cowley School, became interested and allowed the Club the use of the school on two nights a week, one in the gym and one in the hall. The gym was used for football training, basketball and drama. The Club was now catering for youngsters in the age range 11 to 18 years old, and membership stood at approximately 200.

In 1954 Bullingdon Youth Club folded and Cowley Boys Club were offered their premises in a wartime de-contamination centre in the Slade Army Camp. The Club moved into the buildings at 42 Second Avenue later that year. The official opening took place in 1955 by Dr Roger Bannister and named 'Bannister House' after him. The Club was soon open seven nights a week, with a juke-box, television, cafeteria and lounge to complement the sporting activities of football, table-tennis, snooker, darts, basketball, athletics and, with art, drama and carpentry also available, the Club flourished. In nine years some 2,900 boys passed through the Club. Eventually, however, running costs became prohibitive and this, together with dwindling numbers, forced the closure of the Club in 1958.

Johnnie (Lucky) Arnold *Double International Cricket/Football*

John Arnold was born in Temple Road, Cowley on 30 November 1907. He played cricket for Cowley, Oxford City and Oxfordshire, before turning professional with Hampshire County Cricket Club. He was described as being an attractive opening right-hand batsman, particularly effective against spin bowling, right arm slow bowler, excellent deep fielder with strong throw (Cricketers Who's Who). John played for Hampshire CCC between 1929 and 1950 playing 396 matches.

He played in one test match against New Zealand at Lords in 1931, scoring 34 runs in two innings. He scored 1000 runs in a season fourteen times (best 2,261, average 48.10, in 1934).

Hampshire Record

Batting:

Innings	Not Out	Runs	100s	Average
710	45	21,031	37	32.82

His highest score was 227 against Glamorgan in 1932.

Bowling:

Overs	Maidens	Average	Best figures
1181	17	69.52	3-34

Catches taken 184

John was also an accomplished footballer. He played for Cowley Elementary School, Oxford Schools and Oxford City FC. On moving to Hampshire he joined Southampton FC in 1928 and made his league debut against Milwall on 1 April 1929. After playing 110 league and cup games and scoring 46 goals he was transferred, along with Mike Keeping, to Fulham in 1933 for £5,000. Between 1933 and 1939 he made 224 league and cup appearances for Fulham and scored 64 goals. In the 1938-39 season he was awarded his benefit. John's one international cap for England came against Scotland in 1933. The outbreak of war in 1939 effectively put an end to his football career.

George Brown

George Brown was born in Crescent Road, Cowley on 6 October 1887. He was an opening to middle order left-hand batsman, right arm medium pace bowler, wicketkeeper or brilliant close fielder. He played for Hampshire between 1908 and 1933, playing 539 matches.

Batting:	Innings	Not Out	Runs	100s	Average
	1012	52	25,649	37	26.71

Bowling:	Overs	Maidens	Average	Best figures
	18,666	626	29.81	8-55

He took 568 catches and made 78 stumpings

In his day he was one of the most brilliant all-round cricketers ever seen. His batting tended to be inconsistent as well as moving unpredictably from attack to dour defence. He could be given the wicket-keepers job at a moments notice and perform to test match standards, and he was a fair bowler (Cricketers Who's Who). He was described as *"a beautifully built man. He was extraordinarily active and strong and played the game with great enthusiasm and zest"* (The Book of Cricket: Sir Pelman Warner). He made 1,000 runs in a season 11 times; best 2,040 in 1926, average 40.00. The highest of his three double-centuries was 232 not out against Yorkshire in 1920.

He played in 7 test matches for England between 1921 and 1923.

Batting:	Innings	Not Out	Runs	Average	Highest score
	12	2	299	29.90	84

He took 9 catches and made 3 stumpings

George toured with the MCC to the West Indies 1910-11, South Africa 1922-23, to India, Burma and Ceylon 1926-27, and with Tennyson to Jamaica in 1931-32.

Neville Rogers

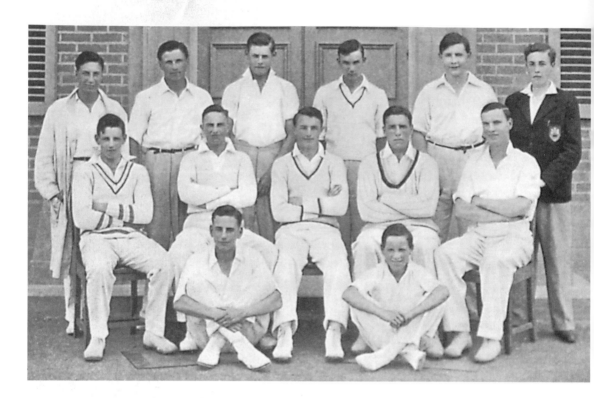

Southfield School First Cricket XI 1935. Left to right back row: W E J Rees, K J Williams, M A Pollard, C M Graham, T A Cox, P A Towl, N A Gidney, A H Reynolds, Neville H Rogers (Capt.), S H Haslehurst, T Dodgson, R A Stevens, D J Walker.

Neville was born 9 March 1918 and the family home was in Crescent Road, Cowley. He attended St James's School in Beauchamp Lane, and later the Municiple Technical School in St Ebbes, and finally Southfield School. While at Southfield he captained the school First XI and, to quote "The Recorder", the school magazine from December 1935 "N H Rogers as captain of the First XI was most industrious and took a keen interest in the school cricket outside his own responsibility. An attractive opening bat who always set a worthy example, and in the field a veritable tower of strength, bringing delight to the spectators and trepidation to the opponents".

On leaving school he worked for Swift & Co, meat wholesalers at the Oxford Railway Station, and played cricket with Oxford City C C and Oxfordshire. He played for Hampshire from 1946 to 1955, recording 285 matches. He was described as a sound opening right-hand batsman, excellent fielder.

Career Batting:	Innings	Not Out	Runs	100s	Average
	528	20	16,056	28	32.04
Bowling:	0-37. Catches 197.				

He hit 1000 runs in a season nine times, once over 2000; 2244 average 40.80 in 1953.

Events and Miscellaneous

These photographs commemorate just a few events, some of which will still be remembered by the people of Cowley.

Watching a hay rick fire at Cowley in the 1890s.

Fire in Crescent Road in the 1920s when the Aslin Blind factory was destroyed. The factory manufactured paper blinds which were very popular as an alternative to lace or linen curtains, hence the name Aslin — as good *as lin*en. The factory was owned by the Sandford Paper Mill. This view is taken from the Cowley Marsh.

The same building c1978, when occupied by a teddy bear factory, Betoys. Mrs Honour's shop, on the corner of Crescent Road and Temple Road, later occupied by Mrs Honour's daughter, Mrs Johnson, and by Mr Giles from about 1950.

Ancient Order of Foresters Juvenile Tea c1925 (OPA).

Armistice Day Parade in Oxford Road c1926 (OPA).

Coronation celebrations 1953. Left to right: Keith Cook, Sheila Eden, Margaret Dykes, the Coronation Queen, Angela Shaw.

Coronation Day celebrations at the Nuffield Arms in Bartholomew Road.

Father Alec Whye on his bicycle, following the crowds. This may have been during Coronation celebrations.

A Coronation Day street party, 2 June 1953, taken in the garden of the Queens Arms in Kelburne Road. Left to right back row: Brenda Hawkes, Brian Sheard, Roger Golder, -?-, Ken Strange, Gill Burr, Charmaine Burr, Angel Goodchild, Maureen Yale, Maureen Hayes. 3rd row: Jacky Yale, Janice Golder, Pat Harding, Trevor Goodchild, Tony Jarvis, Margo Threadkell, Gill Mathews, Susan Newbury, Margaret Edwardson, Ann Brewer. 2nd row: Donald Pocock, Tony Teagel, Derek Burr, Kathleen Edwardson, Daphne Teagel, Angela Bond, Jennifer Hayes, Keith Hayes, Lynda Brewer, Janet Brewer, Kay Emmerton, Wendy Green.

A Coronation Day party in White Road.

Entertainment from the local children.

Children from the Congregational Church Sunday School, and the crowning of the May Queen c1951.

A special occasion for the Nuffield Press, a visit from the Australian Cricket Team in May 1948, seen here with William Morris. Left to right: K A Brown, Doug Ring (behind) Ron Hamence, A James (Masseur), Ron Saggers, Lindsay Hassett, Ian Johnson, Don Tallon, William Morris, Ernie Toshack, William Johnson, Keith Johnson, Neil Harvey, Arthur Morris, Colin McCool, Ray Lindwall, Sam Loxton, W Ferguson (scorer). Also on this tour but not present were: Sid Barnes, Don Bradman and Keith Miller.

Dossets Orchard, 48 Temple Road

An indenture exists, dated 1742, showing the transfer of land from Elizabeth Harper of Kidlington, daughter of Benjamin Dosset butcher and granddaughter of Benjamin Dosset butcher, of Temple Cowley, to Henry Dosset also a butcher.

Sold by auction for £5,500 to Walter Jackson of Wiltshire. At that time was described as a *'charming, little detached modernised XVIIth century cottage residence'* containing beamed and half timbered lounge hall, oak-beamed living room with original stone floor, kitchen and cellar, with 2 bedrooms on first floor and 2 bedrooms on second floor. The total area extended to nearly one acre, *'with a central grass walk running its extreme length and terminating in a full-bearing orchard, producing an abundance of pears, Blenheim, Cox's Orange and other apples, Victoria plums, damsons, yellow cherries, peaches and soft fruit of all descriptions, together with an asparagus bed'*

Holloway Cottage, once stood in its own grounds. It has survived virtually unchanged and is now tucked away amongst modern developments.

Bullingdon Cottage stands sideways on to Salegate Lane. Another typical example of the pretty cottage buildings of Old Cowley.

Crescent Road in the early 1900s. Turners pig farm can be seen in the distance.

Crescent Road in the 1920s. The car is parked outside the premises of the Aslin Blind Company, the manager of which lived in the house on the left hand side.

CRESCENT ROAD,

Cowley.
Continuation of Marsh rd.
to 107 Hollow way.
Map H 8, H 9.
South side.

1A, Corner Stores (W. H. Giles, propr.), grocer & general stores. Tel. 77995
2 Holton Rt. Ernest
4 Hartley Thos
6 Brooks Edwd
8 Preston Mrs. D
10 Hughes Danl
12 Simmons Mrs
14 Cawthorne Mrs
16 Allen Jn
18 Bowell Mrs
20 Hawkins Arth
22 Stanley Jn
24 Thornton Mrs. M
26 Bradbury Harry Jn
28 Clarke Jn
30 Wright's Stores, grocers T N Oxford 77362
32 Babovick N
34 Gibbons Geoffrey
36 Clarke Jn. H
38 Plaisted Mrs
40 Plaisted Thos. Edwd. J
42 Davies Miss M
44 Buckingham Chas. F
46 Biggs Anthony J
48 Carey Jas. J
50 Biggs Thos. Anthony
52 Allen Alfd. Edwd
56 Rogers Mrs. B
64 Baker Fredk. Geo
66 Wicks Albt
74 Wilkinson Wm. Geo
76 Sturges Guy
78 Dobbins Arth. Geo
80 Jones Cyrus L
82 Simpson Matthew
84 Kerry Wm
88 Cook Chas. A
90 Merritt Mrs
92 Baker Chas
94 Minns Eric
96 Bradbury Herbt. Fras
98 Turner Wm. W
98 Turner S. carrier, genl. haulage contr. & pig breeder. T N 77288
104 Plaisted Aubrey Herbt
106 Cleaver Archie H
108 Smith Jas
110 Pullin Herbt. Thos
112 Williams Emrys Jn
114 Bancalari Miss
Maguire Very Rev. Jn J., S.D.B., B.A. (Roman Catholic) (Salesian college)

OXFORD 3½

McKenna Rev. Thos. S.D.B. (Roman Catholic) (Salesian college)
St. Francis of Assisi Roman Catholic Church

SALESIAN COLLEGE (boarding & day Grammar school) (recognised by Ministry of Education) (The Very Rev. John J. Maguire S.D.B., B.A. rector). Telephone, OXFORD 78106/7

.....here is Junction rd......

North side.

1 Davies Miss E
3 Wicks Mrs
5 Davis Arth. E
7 Smart Wm. Jn
9 Dodman Stanley J
11 Green Christphr. R
17 BRADBURY J. H. & SON, builders & decrtrs. Tel. Oxford 78557
17 Bradbury Jn. Hy
19 HILSDON & WILLIAMS, builders & plastering contractors
19 Hilsdon Philip J
21 Pope Jn
23 Lee Mrs
25 Bradbury Mrs. S
27 Comley Ronald
29 Page Mrs
31 Hinton Harold J
33 Wright Ernest A
35 Thompson Dennis
37 Lee Edwd
39 Barden Ernest G. grocer & provision mer
41 Newell Miss
43 Harrison Mrs
45 Johnson Jn. car hire service
47 Winter Jn
49 Talbot Leslie R
51 Allen Jn
53 Johnson Stephen Edwin
65 Costello Michl. D
71 Pinkney Jas
75 Mathers D. C
77 Harrop Douglas Hy
79 King Mrs
81 Smith Percy W
85 Harris Arth
87 Packham Stanley
89 Gardner Mrs. I. R
91 Osborne Mrs
95 Chew Harold
97 Lambert Miss
99 Spiller Wm

103 Roberts Capt. Frank M
107
109 Hawtin Crescens M
111 Lester Chas. W
113 Keen Harry Leslie
115 Rowles Denis
117 Jeffery Wm
119 McCarthy Patrick
121 Brooks Arth. W
123 Cripps Percvl. F
125 Brooks Arth. F
127 Job's Dairy, dairymen
127 King Geo
129 Morris Motors Athletic & Social Club & Grounds) (J. A. T. Boulger, sec.; J. Asling, steward). Telephone, Oxford 770641 & 77524
143 Foster Albt. Jn
145 Foulks Wm
163 **HARRISON & MOULDER**, church woodworkers & furnishers. Tel. 78430 & 77479
165 Kinkaid Wm
169 Hays Edwd. D
171 Culhane Denis

CRICK ROAD,

St. Giles'.

From 17 Bradmore road to Fyfield road. Map D 5.

North side.

Caccia Anthony M., C.B., M.V.O., M.A. (Elsmere)
1 Adams Jas. V
2B, Irving Harry Munroe N. H., M.A., D.Phil., D.Sc
2C, Withycombe Miss E. G
2A, Hayward Percy G
3 Gifford Miss M. J. Tel. 57783
3 Porter Miss M. W., D.Sc
4 Tustian Miss E. A
5A, Thompson Mrs. C
5B, Campbell Miss M
6 (flat 1) Burchett Peter A
6 (flat 2) Procter Mrs. P. M
6 (flat 3) Thompson Kenneth D
6 (flat 4) Cuthbertson Miss B
6 (flat 5) Davis Mrs. H. W. C
6 (flat 6) Walters Miss E

Residents of Crescent Road from Kellys Directory 1949.

Aerial view of the new Cowley Centre c1964. John Allen's factory and playing field are on the left and mid-distance on the right can be seen the new Cowley Community Centre (white roof) with the old Bedford House just in front. This is now the site of Cowley